Teachers and Parents: An Adult-to-Adult Approach

Teachers and Parents: An Adult-to-Adult Approach

Dorothy Rich

nea PROFESSIONAL LIBRARY
National Education Association
Washington, D.C.

This manuscript is an adaptation of *Between Teachers and Parents: A New Partnership*, which was produced by Dorothy Rich Associates, Inc., under a U.S. Department of Education contract to Decision Resources Corporation.

Note

The opinions expressed in this publication should not be construed as representing the policy or position of the National Education Association. Materials published as part of the Parent Involvement Series are intended to be discussion documents for teachers who are concerned with specialized interests of the profession.

Library of Congress Cataloging-in-Publication Data

Rich, Dorothy.
    Teachers and parents.

(Parent involvement series)
    Bibliography: p.
    1. Home and school—United States.   2. Parent-teacher
relationships—United States.   3. Education—
United States—Parent participation.   I. Title.
II. Series.
LC225.R53 1987   371.1'03   87-20231
ISBN 0-8106-0277-6

CONTENTS

The Author

Dorothy Rich is the founder and president of the Home and School Institute. A nonprofit educational organization based in Washington, D.C., HSI works to link the resources of the school, the home, and the community for student academic achievement and school success. Since 1964 HSI has developed an innovative approach to community involvement in education by providing a structured tutoring role for the family that complements but does not duplicate the work of the school. HSI developed the Teacher-Parent Partnership Project for NEA, as well as the NEA Professional Library multimedia training program *Schools and Parents United: A Practical Approach to Student Success.*

The Advisory Panel

Clara Elmore-Bain, Assistant Professor of Reading, Savannah State College, Georgia

Cheryl Fant Bannerman-Williams, Information-Media Specialist, Memphis City Schools, Tennessee

J. Merrell Hansen, Director of Secondary Education, Provo School District, Utah

Jack Hartjes, fifth grade teacher, St. Joseph's School, Pierz, Minnesota

Michael H. Jessup, Professor of Education, Towson State University, Maryland

Joyce L. May, Chair of English Department, Sunset High School, Beaverton, Oregon

Chapter 1
INTRODUCTION

QUESTION: Why should teachers take time to work with parents when they need to focus on children?

ANSWER: Because children's achievement depends on parent-teacher cooperation.

There is today a unique and opportune convergence of forces and needs upon families and teachers. For example—

- Teachers are realizing more than ever that it is vital to work in partnership with parents and the community.
- A growing research base is affirming the impact of families as educators of their children.
- There is strong public interest in self-help initiatives rather than in waiting for schools and teachers to take care of family needs.

For children to achieve in school, they need family involvement and reinforcement at home. This is such a truism that it is usually followed by the words "of course." The reality, however, is that this truism has somehow been overlooked, especially in recent years. In the effort to professionalize education and in the growth of schooling, the role of the family has been forgotten. While the needs of children have been a major educational focus, the needs of parents have received little or no attention. (*Note*: "family" involvement and "parent" involvement are used interchangeably in these pages.)

9

This publication outlines for teachers reasons for working with parents. It presents a sampling of practical strategies that teachers can use to foster parent competence and responsibility in the education of their children. And it also contains answers to some of the questions teachers are asking such as— How can I get my students' parents to pay attention? How can I get parents to visit the school? How can I get parents positively involved in their children's education? The basic theme underscoring these answers is that family support can best be realized when teachers pay attention not only to children but also to parents.

This publication does not deal with such problems as child abuse and neglect, student pregnancy, drug and alcohol abuse, or eating disorders. For information on these topics, see the NEA Combat Series—*How Schools Can Help Combat Child Abuse and Neglect*, (30)* *How Schools Can Help Combat Student Pregnancy* (7), *How Schools Can Help Combat Student Drug and Alcohol Abuse* (31), and *How Schools Can Help Combat Student Eating Disorders* (20), and/or contact the NEA Professional Library (1201 16th Street, NW, Washington, D.C. 20036).

Earlier strategies for involving parents are no longer successful. The employed mother or single parent is not able to attend the 2 P.M. meeting at school or to chaperone the class field trip. Old problems are made different by new conditions, especially by changes in the family. These changing conditions demand different home-school approaches.

THE IMPORTANCE OF FAMILY INVOLVEMENT

Family demographics affects the work of the school. Teachers today need to find ways to deal constructively with

---

*Numbers in parentheses appearing in the text refer to the Bibliography beginning on page 108.

the fact that the majority of mothers are in the work force and a growing number of children are living in single-parent homes. (Chapter 7 presents an overview of the impact of single-parent households on student achievement.) While not all the answers or even all the questions are yet known, enough information is available for teachers to initiate effective programs with today's families. In order to work with their children's school, however, parents must have their own needs met. These include reassurance and being talked to as adults.

This new approach goes beyond traditional rhetoric about parent support for the school such as attending PTA meetings and making sure that children do homework. It focuses on the need for the schools to support the educational role of the parents. This role, recently rediscovered by research, emphasizes what parents can do at home with children and is highly significant in children's achievement (28).

A KEY QUESTION

The key question for teachers to address is: What do I have to do to relate to and connect with parents that is different from what I do with children? To date, most teachers have not had training or experience in working with parents. Moreover, the teacher-parent relationship is not a simple one. As Roland Barth, school principal and author, has observed:

One might expect that sharing a daily preoccupation with the same children would form a common bond, bringing principal, teacher, and parents together. Unfortunately, this bond seldom develops naturally or spontaneously. We school people need help in finding ways to work cooperatively with parents; and parents badly need assistance in translating their basic caring into actions that will improve the situation for their children, the school and themselves. (1)

11

The encouraging news is that teachers and parents can take these actions, using the relevant experience and knowledge gained in the past two decades. This monograph is, in essence, an accelerated teacher-training session in the how-to's of working with parents as adult partners in the education of their children.

CLASSROOM BENEFITS OF FAMILY INVOLVEMENT

Evidence indicates that parent involvement—

- Raises the academic achievement of students.
- Improves the attitudes and performance of children in school.
- Helps parents understand the work of the schools.
- Builds school-community relationships in an ongoing, problem-preventing way (9).

These results do not occur immediately. While there is still more to learn about family involvement, enough is now known about its benefits to prompt more teachers to use it to support and extend the impact of classroom instruction.

FAMILY INVOLVEMENT TODAY

The traditional form of family involvement of the last two decades has been the advisory council with parents acting in an advisory capacity. Effective family involvement appropriate for today's families is different. The advisory role, which may have been a relevant and useful model at the time of its design, is no longer the most appropriate involvement method. Even the role of classroom volunteer, which was highly lauded, is of limited impact in comparison to the role of the family in education. Working at home with the child reinforces and supplements the work of the school.

Traditionally, families have been identified by deficits, with the school acting in a compensatory role. Effective involvement today should be based on a nondeficit view of families. The position of this publication, based on experience with thousands of families, is that there are strengths in every family that can be mobilized into effective educational action. Good involvement provides learning strategies for families to use at home. These reinforce but do not duplicate the work of the school. In other words, good involvement assigns educational responsibilities to the family.

THE ROLES OF TEACHERS AND PARENTS

This monograph recommends an involvement of the home that extends the work of the school. Such an involvement is based on the different strengths of the home and the classroom. Although the roles of parents and teachers are different, they are complementary. The family is in the ideal position to prepare for, expand, and extend the work of the school. In addition to traditional homework, there is also the opportunity for families to engage in individualized give-and-take with students at "teachable moments" that teachers can only dream about. Ways for teachers to teach families how to take advantage of these moments are outlined in these pages.

Despite the changes in today's families, parents continue to care about their children and teachers to care about the achievement of their students. Both have more abilities and potential to do a successful job than ever before.

Chapter 2
NEW ROLES, NEW FACTS ABOUT FAMILIES AND TEACHERS

It has been traditional to talk about the need for family support of the school. This has usually been defined through such activities as voting for the school budget, supporting the school as an institution, and volunteering efforts in support of the school's activities. Today, this definition of parent involvement is inadequate as an approach to home-school relations. Research tells us that the home is a vital educational institution: every school depends on the input from the home. Children's motivation to learn and to keep on learning depends on the attitudes they bring to the classroom from the living room (33).

Most schools, however, have not yet worked with the home in a concerted, systematic manner. In fact, reform reports have not addressed this rediscovered dimension of the family in education. The report of the National Commission on Excellence in Education, for example, centers almost exclusively on the school. It addresses parents only in a postscript:

> As surely as you are your children's most important teachers, your children's ideas about education and its significance begin with you . . . Moreover, you bear a responsibility to participate actively in your children's education. (22)

These are good words. But the report does not specify what is included in that parental responsibility nor what is expected of teachers in working with parents. This monograph focuses on these joint responsibilities.

THE FAMILY TODAY

Today's teachers must work with a new kind of family. The majority of mothers hold jobs outside the home and single parenting is on the increase. It is predicted that by the year 2000, 50 percent of all children will have lived, at least for a time, in a single-parent household (3). But, even under the contraints of limited time and financial pressures, today's parents still care about and value their children's schooling. After years of heavy dependence on the school to do everything, the public appears ready to assume more responsibility for what is happening to children. Recent Gallup Polls, for example, cited lack of discipline as a major school problem. When asked for the cause of the school's discipline problems, the public, including parents, placed blame on the home (26).

The optimistic news is that most parents today are better educated than those of previous decades, and many are seeking involvement in the education of their children. These parents may not come to the traditional meetings, but studies and experience indicate that they are interested in ways to help their own children. What they want and respond to are ways to become involved in and linked to their own children's school achievement (29).

TEACHING TODAY

Teachers today are paying the price exacted by the pervasive myth of the school as superinstitution. Starting in the late 1950s, schools were increasingly expected to assume more responsibilities. There were placed on a pedestal and then criticized for not performing miracles.

Just as family life has changed, so has the role of the teacher. The knowledge resulting from technology and the information revolution is reaching everyone at once—in

15

kitchens as well as in classrooms. This change means that teachers now play a new role in pulling together knowledge and resources both inside and outside the school. It requires that teachers have the training and the ability to work with a variety of educational resources, including the family.

There has been little, if any, discussion to date of this major change in the teacher's role. Chapters 4, 5, and 6 contain strategies for teachers now facing this exciting new leadership prospect.

THE OLD HOME-SCHOOL TIES

Over the years parents have been involved in the work of the school in several different ways. A brief summary of the pros and cons of these methods follows.

Parents as Volunteers—Volunteerism offers extra person power in the classroom. Managed effectively, it can give teachers more teaching time. At its best, this method provides active roles for parents, but volunteers help students in general, not necessarily their own children.

Parents as Receivers of Information About the School—Parent-school communication usually comes in the form of report cards, conferences, and newsletters to keep parents informed. Most of this communication is initiated by the school, however, with parents playing relatively passive roles.

Parents as Policymakers at the School—Policymaking usually takes the form of parent advisory committees. However, relatively few working parents today can participate in such committees. A major study of parent involvement in federal programs such as ESEA Chapter I, the Emergency School Aid

Act, found that the advisory council, which had taken so much school effort, was not an effective model for eliciting parent involvement (5).

Parents Working with Their Own Children at Home—Parent education and training involves teaching parents how to improve their family life and/or how to work with their children. Of all the models identified, this is the one that offers the most substantive research to date with findings most directly linked to children's achievement. It is the most appropriate model for the widespread involvement of families and the effective use of teacher time and energy. (For a detailed discussion of the new emphasis on traditional parent roles, see Appendix A.)

WHAT DOES RESEARCH TELL US?

The noted social scientist Urie Bronfenbrenner has determined that the active involvement of the family reinforces and helps sustain the effect of school programs. (2) The late Ira Gordon's research, especially in the Follow Through program, concluded that all forms of parent involvement help, but that the more comprehensive the involvement (e.g., the more roles parents can play in a school) and the longer this involvement lasts, the more effective it will be (12).

It is increasingly clear from research that priority attention should be given to participation that directly involves parents in the education of their own child. This is often referred to as the "parent-as-tutor" approach. The reasons for this position are twofold. First, it is the approach that a continuing line of research indicates is most directly linked to improved academic achievement. The study, *Parent Involvement in Compensatory Education Programs*, assessed the major models of parent involvement. In general, the evidence supported the participation of parents as tutors of their children. "As a

17

group," say the authors, "the programs involving parents as tutors consistently produced significant immediate gains in children's IQ scores, and seemed to alter in a positive direction the teaching behavior of parents" (11).

The second reason for this position is that it offers the greatest opportunity for widespread and sustained involvement. Programs that require attendance at meetings or involvement in school activities during the day will necessarily have limited participation. The need to reach out to single parents and to families in which both parents work concerns teachers. Furthermore, this approach appeals to the most basic motivation for involvement—the desire to help one's child do better in school.

Studies since the 1970s at all grade levels have shown that schooling is markedly enhanced by family involvement (6). It is not clear therefore why educational reform continues to focus almost exclusively on the school, when the family is such a vital and determining educational force.

Teachers are beginning to be asked for their opinions. For example, David Williams evaluated parent involvement by elementary teachers in a six-state southeastern regional survey. Teachers in his study were not enthusiastic about parent participation in curriculum development, instruction, or school governance. They supported other forms of parent involvement, such as assisting with homework or tutoring children, but felt that they should give parents ideas about how to help. They also noted that their own schools did not usually provide opportunities for parents and teachers to work together (35).

An accompanying survey of elementary principals produced similar results. In this study, principals valued parent participation in children's home learning for several reasons: it helps schools, reinforces school learning, and is within parents' capabilities (35).

THE QUESTION AND THE ANSWER

The question now should be asked: Has this evidence changed the work of most schools in the ways they relate to the family and the home? The answer to date is: Somewhat, but not enough. The current initiative by schools to form partnerships with business is a move in the right direction. For example, a specific business works with a particular school, providing clasroom volunteers and student internships. However, most of these efforts are focused on the high school years. To reach the widest number of children in earlier school years, it is vital for schools to connect with the family.

In fact, this is a time of opportunity when everyone agrees that education is a priority concern and something must be done. The U.S. Department of Education has talked about a reemphasis on families. The National Education Association has initiated the Teacher-Parent Partnership Project. It is an ideal time to link the resources of the home and the school to build a strong, shared responsibility for children's education.

Chapter 3
WHAT DO TEACHERS AND PARENTS WANT?—BUILDING TRUST

To an extent perhaps not possible before, teachers and parents, who play different roles in the same children's lives, are human beings with similar problems. Both teachers and parents go dancing, get married, have children, need child care, and in many cases divorce. With common concerns, teachers and parents have greater potential for understanding and meeting each others' needs. This chapter focuses on how teachers can develop an effective partnership between the home and the school by responding to parents' needs.

WHAT DO TEACHERS WANT?

What are the stated needs of teachers and the benefits they can expect to receive from parent involvement programs? The National Education Association, through its Nationwide Teacher Opinion Polls, surveys teachers regularly on a variety of issues (23). Among the questions asked have been some on the relationship between home and school. The responses offer useful insights into teachers' perceptions of the importance of the home to their work.

Student Behavior—Teachers were given a long list of conditions that have been connected with student misbehavior in schools. Of all the factors listed, including overcrowded classes and lack of support from principals, the two rated highest by teachers were "Irresponsible Parents" and "Unsatisfactory Home Conditions."

Home-School Interaction—When asked in the same poll if they thought more home-school interaction was needed, 93.6 percent of the teachers responded yes, 6.4 percent responded no (23).

Importance of the Home—Teachers were also asked: "Recognizing that both homelife and schools are important, which of the two do you think is more important in determining whether or not a child achieves academically?" Homelife was chosen by 87.6 percent of the teachers, school by 12.4. percent (23).

The fact that teachers consider homelife so important can also be seen as a recognition of the significance of the home as an educational environment—a recognition that teachers can now mobilize and act upon.

PARENT INVOLVEMENT BENEFITS FOR TEACHERS

Parent involvement programs help teachers receive higher ratings from parents. In Maryland, researcher Joyce Epstein found that—

> Parents who participated in involvement programs were more positive about the teacher's interpersonal skills, and rated the teacher higher in overall teaching ability. . . . In other words, teachers who work at parent involvement are considered better teachers than those who remain more isolated from the families of the children they teach. (9)

Epstein analyzed survey responses to see how teacher practices involving parents affected what parents did or said:

> Results show that parents whose children's teachers were leaders in parent involvement were more likely than other parents to report: they recognized that the teacher worked

21

hard to interest parents in the instructional program; they received most of their ideas for home involvement from the teachers; they felt that they should help their children at home; they understood more this year than last about what their child was being taught in school. (9)

This research suggests that important consequences for student achievement, attitudes, and behavior occur when teachers make parent involvement part of their regular teaching practices. Students report that they have more positive attitudes toward school, more regular homework habits, and the teacher knows the family.

The evaluation report for Year I of the Home and School Institute's (HSI) multilingual home activity project, *In Any Language: Parents Are Teachers* (32), reported the following additional payoffs for teachers:

For the teachers, the major benefits have been increased parental involvement with their child's school experiences. The teachers report that more parents came to school conferences than would come to school functions and programs, and more parents would contact the school regarding their child's absence from school or aspects of their child's school work. (32)

As one teacher said to the evaluator: "This project has helped pull parents into the school. The parents of my kids have been unusually involved this year, not just in coming to school for programs and parent conferences but they're calling more and sending more notes. I also sense they are looking at the homwork more than last year."

These findings are reiterated by teachers to the NEA/HSI Teacher-Parent Partnership Project (24):

"The children enjoyed extra attention at home and school."
"Children had a sense of pride in accomplishment."
"The project provided quality time for students."
"The activities meshed with county curriculum goals."
"Positive communication was developed among teachers."

"Overwhelmingly, parents felt more positive about the teachers and school as a result of the project."

Finding ways for schools to establish family support in education is strategic use of scarce public resources. A minor input of school staff time and materials makes a major output of parent support possible. Getting help from families means building a stronger educational and political base. To obtain this help, however, teachers may first have to overcome a major occupational hazard.

A Pitfall for Teachers

It is an occupational hazard—teachers tend to be "teacherish." This is a useful attribute for work with children, but it can be ruinous in the parent-teacher relationship. For example, when I recently asked a woman's group how teachers treat parents, their responses—some from teachers themselves—were instructive:

"She talked to me as though I were an idiot. Why do teachers explain things over and over?"

"Teachers think parents have nothing else to do except pay attention to their assignment for the kids. Sometimes those assignments are meant more for the parents than for the child. When kids are assigned to cook French food, who do teachers think is buying the fancy ingredients and actually cooking the food? I hardly have time to cook our regular meals!"

"Teachers give parents orders: they treat us like kids. They tell me, 'Have your child here at such and such a time looking such and such way!' They don't ask for my opinion."

"Take the issue of homework. Are we supposed to help or not? Teachers say no, and I am ready not to help. But then my youngster brings home an unrealistic assignment that he can't do alone, like setting up a fancy science fair experiment overnight. It's supposed to be the child's assignment. He says all the other parents do these for their kids. What am I supposed to do?"

These college-educated parents are expressing their own needs as adults in working with teachers and schools. Their concern about their children's schooling is high, but their own needs are also real. The complaints of less formally educated parents may sound a little different, but they are basically the same: "Teachers don't listen to us." "They feel we have nothing to offer." "They don't respect us."

Respect is a key theme that runs through the majority of parents' comments about teachers. Parents very much need and want teachers' respect. Conversely, a list of justifiable teacher complaints about parents could be compiled. The focus of this monograph, however, is on what teachers can do, using the complaints as clues, to involve parents in positive action on behalf of children's education. The basic ingredients in a good parent-teacher relationship are understanding and trust. Implicit in such a relationship is the mutual respect of both parties. The remainder of this chapter focuses on understanding and relating to parents as adults; it outlines specific strategies for teachers to use in establishing greater parent trust.

WHAT DO PARENTS WANT?

Parents have needs that teachers must try to meet. After years of being told that they don't know "the right way" to raise their children, parents need to have their confidence restored. Teachers will have to convince parents to believe in themselves and once again regard themselves as significant "educators" of their childrun.

A Pitfall for Parents

Underneath most parents is a student—someone who went to school, sometimes happily, sometimes unhappily. What often happens when the parent-as-adult returns to school, or has dealings with teachers, is that the parent as child/student returns. Many parents still enter school buildings flooded with old memories, angers, and disappointments. Their stomachs churn and flutter with butterflies, not because of what is happening today with their own children, but because of outdated memories and behaviors of the past.

Consequently, teachers may have trouble getting these parents to act like the mature adults they are. Just as it is vital that teachers treat parents as adults, parents have to be helped to recognize their own pitfalls that may prevent them from acting like adults in school. One way for teachers to address these ghosts is to spend a few minutes talking with parents about their own school experiences. This helps to separate earlier reactions from what is happening with their own child in the present.

PARENTS AS ADULT LEARNERS

In order to reach and teach parents today, teachers must work with them as adults, as people with their own learning needs. Adults learn differently from children. Making this transition to working with adults is not easy for teachers who have received little or no training in this area. The tips that follow are useful for contact between parents and teachers and between teachers and their own supervisors. Many teachers feel that they themselves are not treated as adult learners by their own administrators.

Successful teaching, especially with adults, provides people with experiences they seek, can accept, and will grow from, rather than with situations they want to avoid and will resist.

Implications for Teachers

Teachers can apply Maslow's five "universal desires" (19) to the parent-teacher relationship as follows:

25

1. *Recognition*—Let parents know that they are significant educators of their children. Share with them some examples from the research; give them a greater sense of their importance in their children's lives.

2. *Affection*—Let parents know that you understand and know personally how difficult it is to be a parent today and to juggle the tasks of family and job. Share an experience or two that shows that all parents, including teachers as parents themselves, have similar problems and joys.

3. *Power*—Let parents know that the school believes that every family has strengths, such as the parents' love for their children. These strengths can be mobilized to help the family, teachers, and children. This is a "nondeficit" view of families. (See Appendix D for a discussion of the characteristics of effective families.)

4. *New Experiences*—Encourage parents to try new teaching activities at home and enjoy the real thrill that comes in teaching—seeing children learn! (These activities are described in Chapter 4.) Share with families home teaching ideas that are nonthreatening and easy to do, such as using the laundry to teach reading classification skills to young children, and using newspaper ads to teach older youngsters how to find the best buys in foods.

5. *Security*—Let parents know that they are needed and wanted. Try to avoid making them feel guilty for not having been involved before or for being unable to attend school events during the workday. Because of their own school experience, many parents start with basic insecurity about school. You can reduce this feeling by sharing as much information as possible about how the school works, and about teachers' concerns for parent needs.

ADULT LEARNING CHARACTERISTICS

Knowles identifies at least four adult learning characteristics relevant to the parent-teacher relationship:

- *Self-Direction*—Adults tend to know what they need to learn.
- *Life Experience*—Adults expect to use their experiences in addressing problems.
- *Problem Centered*—Adults learn best around life problems rather than "subjects." Adults want and need practical solutions.
- *Self-Evaluation*—Adults not only are ready to determine their own goals (self-direction), but they also want feedback on how well they are progressing to meet these goals.

Implications for Teachers

The following examples illustrate the application of these adult learning characteristics to the parent-teacher relationship:

- *Self-Direction*—To avoid "talking down" to parents, teachers can encourage parents to diagnose their own learning needs. For example, instead of telling parents what they need to learn, teachers can ask what parents think they need to learn in order to work with their children and the school.
- *Experience*— Parents hope teachers will respect the family's own life experience. Failure by teachers to use this experience is equivalent to rejection of parents as persons. When inviting parents for a conference or a meeting, teachers should plan for active involvement, not passive learning. Encourage meetings in which parents talk with and help one another. Self-help groups are an

ideal way to place appropriate responsibilities on parents, thus removing them from the already overburdened teachers.

- *Problem Centered*—Adults are far more ready to tackle specific, rather than general, problems. For example, parents want to know about their own child, not about children in general. Teachers should give parents facts about their child and expect parent problem-solving help. Is the child having trouble with homework? With friends? What can we do about it? Parents have a stake in solving these problems and need the opportunity to get involved.

- *Self-Evaluation*—Adults tend to be more interested in feedback than in grades. Teachers can help parents evaluate how well they are doing at home by sharing information on how their children are doing in school.

The foregoing tips can help teachers build on parents' strengths. In this way, parents gain confidence to do what must be done to help the school and to help their children.

Chapter 4
EDUCATIONAL RESPONSIBILITIES GO HOME

Families need to know about and take responsibility for enhancing the education of their children. The family-as-educator role outlined in this monograph differs from home schooling; it also differs from the teacher's role in school. Family-as-educator refers to the informal but strong role parents play in preparing children for school and in reinforcing and expanding the work of the school through learning experiences at home. (See Appendix B for a description of Mega-Skills™, basic skills that children need to learn at home that are reinforced in the classroom.) These can range from such activities as helping children to organize time and materials for school to using the supermarket and gas station as places for reading and arithmetic practice.

The parent involvement approach recommended here extends the work of the school but does not duplicate it. It is based on the complementary but different strengths of the home and the school. Parents want to help their children, but even well-educated parents do not always feel they know how. They look to the schools for help. In fact,. the family is in an ideal position to prepare for, expand, and extend the work of the school. In order to ensure the success of their work, teachers must take advantage of this situation.

HOME LEARNING ACTIVITIES

For two decades, home learning activities have been a core component in all Home and School Institute (HSI) programs for families. They provide a structured tutoring role for the family that deliberately does not duplicate the work of the school.

These activities are designed to help children become more academically motivated and self-disciplined, to provide a framework for parents to work with their children, and to build stronger community and parental support for teachers and the role of teaching.

The activities are not designed to help a child pass tomorrow's test. They are family activities to help children feel more successful by doing a real-life task together with an adult. For example, a child may learn to answer the telephone with more confidence, make a wiser decision about buying clothing, or talk with parents about what to watch on TV. Reading, writing, and arithmetic are part of all of the activities, but they are not workbook exercises. They are real-life experiences.

In the course of a semester, classroom teachers send one activity each week home with students. Together, children and their parents complete them. Parents return feedback sheets that indicate they have completed the activity—an interaction that increases communication among all participants.

Activity Structure

Each activity is produced on single sheets of paper and contains the following parts:

- *Why Do It*—explains the purpose of the activity and the skills children will learn.
- *Materials*—lists things needed. These are everyday items found around the house and in the neighborhood— magazines, newspapers, pens, pencils, paper, etc.
- *How to Do It*—gives steps parents and children take to complete the activity.

- *More Ideas*—suggests several new ideas to extend children's skills. This section is different from the main activity; its suggestions may be easier or more difficult.
- *Helpful Hint*—offers tips to parents on how to make the activity work easily and suggests special ways to tell a child "You've done a good job!"

The activities are designed to be accomplished easily and briefly in the home and to require no more than 15 to 30 minutes to complete. It is recommended that families complete only one activity per week. The goal is to build systematic family involvement without overburdening parents.

Example

The sample activity that appears on page 32 is taken from the HSI Arlington Public Schools PACT Project (1987).

RESEARCH ON THE USE
OF HOME LEARNING ACTIVITIES

Data from the use of HSI Home Learning activities are very encouraging. Perhaps most important is the finding that families do these activities with their children, voluntarily and delightedly, pleased with themselves as teachers and with their children as learners. Although tutorial behaviors and roles have been most commonly associated with educated parents and middle-class lifestyles, R. J. Dave found that research and the experience of many programs working with disadvantaged and minority families confirm that educational attainment need not be a barrier to parents in tutoring their children (8). (For brief descriptions of the many kinds of HSI programs, as well as a summary of what teachers and parents say about these programs, see Appendix C.)

HSI projects have served low socioeconomic families in the District of Columbia, Michigan, Maryland, California, South

31

Doing It!—Setting Up a Homework System

Why Do It
This activity helps children set up an easy homework chart that enables them to jot down daily what has to be done.

Materials—Paper, marker, clock

How to Do It
- You and your child make note of the dates when your child will have homework. You can get this information from your child's teacher.
- Set up a homework chart. Use a sturdy, large-sized piece of paper that can be posted on a wall. Here's a sample.

Days	English	Math	Social Studies	Science
Monday				
Tuesday				
etc.				

- Attach a colored marker or pen to the chart so that it is always handy.
- Each day after school, have your child check off the homework assignments. Your child circles the check to show completed homework.

Another Idea
Let your child figure out how long it takes to complete assignments. Don't include interruptions such as telephone calls or TV time. Keep a clock nearby.

Helpful Hint
Talk about each assignment with your child after it's completed. Was it difficult? Easy? Would your child like to know more? Plan followup trips to museums and libraries.

Carolina, and Virginia, as well as special education and multilingual populations. Family participation in six of these programs is briefly summarized below:

- *Project Help*—After using eight home learning activities, first grade children scored significantly higher on standardized reading tests than the control group. Project HELP first grade Title I children, who in the beginning had the lowest scores of all groups studied, after a program of learning activities sent home weekly, made gains in reading equal to those of the children in other groups who started at higher levels (4).

- *Parent-Teacher Partnership*—Using the HSI model in special education in the inner city, this project found a highly significant increase in children's reasoning skills as well as an increase of over three grade levels in visual-aural skills (17). The majority of special education youngsters who participated are now mainstreamed into regular classrooms.

- *Project AHEAD* (Accelerating Home Education and Development)—Developed for the Southern Christian Leadership Conference West, this project serves 5,000 children, primarily Black and Hispanic, in grades K–3, with a parent-to-parent approach. Results show significant increases in second and third grade scores on the California Tests of Basic Skills. Ninety-seven percent of the parents indicated they wanted to stay in the program, which has been adopted by the Los Angeles Unified School District (27).

- *Families Learning Together*—This program for simultaneous adult and child learning served families with children in grades K–6. The participation rate was 77 percent of the total school population. Ninety-eight

33

percent of the parents said they themselves acquired useful skills and knowledge from the program. And 98.5 percent said they felt more confident in working with their own child at home (16).

- *Multilingual School Success Project*—A series of family learning activities was developed and translated into Spanish, Vietnamese, Khmer, and Lao for families of children in grades 4–6. The data show a family participation rate of nearly 90 percent across a full semester of activities (32).

- *National Education Association/HSI Teacher-Parent Partnership Project*—In 1984–85, 140 elementary schools in 10 states were involved in this project, with over 6,000 students voluntarily participating. Families at all the sites answered questions about their involvement in the program. For example, 91 percent of the parents said the activity was used in the home; 99 percent thought the activity helped the parent spend enjoyable time with his/her child; 98 percent felt his/her child learned something useful; and 99 percent thought the activity would be helpful to other parents (24). Grandparents and other adults were also encouraged to participate in the project. Certificates of achievement were distributed by local associations to families who completed the activities.

In short, this field experience indicates that family concern for education can be readily translated into practical support for children and for schools.

TRANSLATING RESEARCH INTO ACTION

Joyce Epstein's studies not only support home learning activities as having positive impact upon achievement and school performance, but they also provide insight into their feasibility. Testifying before a Congressional Committee, Epstein stated:

> Almost all parents believe parent involvement is important, but most parents cannot or do not become involved at school. Over 40 percent of the mothers in this sample worked full time and 18 percent part time. In contrast, almost all parents were involved at least once in a while in learning activities at home. Over 85 percent reported that they spent 15 minutes or more helping their child at home when asked to do so by the teacher and that they would spend more time if shown how to help.... If teachers had to choose only one policy to stress, these results suggest that the most payoff for the most parents and students will come from teachers involving parents in helping their children in learning activities at home. (9)

Chapter 5
PARENT INVOLVEMENT IN ACTION: WHAT EVERY TEACHER CAN DO

"Planning" is the operational word in effective parent involvement programs. Small-scale, well-planned activities are more doable; they can also be far more effective than those that are large-scale and grandiose. This chapter briefly describes a variety of specific practical activities to strengthen the partnership between the home and the school. Each one follows an easy-to-do plan that can be adapted to meet local school-community needs. The activities cost little or nothing; they use readily available, inexpensive materials; and they require a minimum expenditure of time and effort. All have been tried and tested.

These activities fall into four categories: "Winning Ways in Elementary School," "If You're Having a Meeting, Try These Tips," "Information Sharing—Good at Any Grade," and "Parent Involvement—Even in Secondary School." They focus on parent needs for—

- Social and emotional support for building self-esteem and for dealing with the demands of parenthood
- Information about schooling and child care issues, including latchkey child self-care concerns
- Actual involvement in their children's education
- Interaction with teachers and the school.

In meeting these needs, teachers will receive in exchange the support from parents that makes it possible for the school to do a more effective job.

36

WINNING WAYS IN ELEMENTARY SCHOOL

Feature Family of the Week

Set up a family bulletin board. This "brings" family members into school without their physical appearance. Each week, each class selects one family to feature. Students compile information about family members and mount it on a poster with family snapshots.

Information for the bulletin board can come from a family file assembled at the beginning of the school year, with each family jotting down as much information as it wants to share—such as the parents' jobs, family pets and hobbies.

Welcome new students by taking snapshots of them and posting these, along with a map showing their homes, on the bulletin board. After the display, the photos can be sent home to parents in "welcome folders."

Star of the Day

Make every child feel happy and send good feelings home to the family. Choose a different child each day to be "Star of the Day," to hear from classmates what is good about him/herself. Allow five minutes for the award ceremony. Classmates sit in a circle and take turns saying something positive about the star. Record all statements. For example: Mary said, "I like the way John smiles." Send these comments home with the "star" at the end of the day.

Older children can use "star time" for writing practice. Each student places a positive note in the "star's" mailbox sometime during the day. At the end of the day, the notes can be shared.

We Miss Your Child

Print cards or mimeographed sheets with "We Miss You" and an appropriate illustration. The cards might be an art class project. Send cards home when a child has been absent three or more days. With it include a personal note from the class.

These cards tell children and their parents that they are missed. For students who are absent for extended periods, a weekly log of class activities and tape-recorded messages from classmates can also be sent home.

Grandparents and Neighbors

These very special people can play an important role in the school. Check with a local senior center for names you can contact. Extend personalized visiting cards. Have these cards available also for neighbors who can be invited in to see the school.

Do a little talent scouting. At the beginning of the school year, send home an information collection resource form on which grandparents can list their jobs, interests, or particular skills. These forms can be delivered by the children, and the information can be used throughout the year. If grandparents live nearby or come on a visit, they can be invited to school to demonstrate a craft, give a travel report on a country being studied, or conduct a class tour through their place of work.

Resource Person of the Week

Set up a Resource Person of the Week poster in the teachers' lounge. This can include a photo, some background materials, information on how the person can help teachers, and ways to contact her/him. School personnel can also be highlighted in this way.

Honoring Parents: "Million-Dollar Checks"

Make sure your families know how much the school appreciates them. Teachers can do it with an end-of-year tea, with certificates, a commendation, and "a million-dollar check" made out to each family. What is important is that each school shows that it cares about its families.

The Telephone Connection

A telephone call to a student's home need not turn into a source of dread for the teacher—an interminable conversation at the end of a long day. Teachers who have mastered the art of a quick, polite call can do it in two minutes or less: "Just wanted to let you know that Johnny's fighting has stopped," or "Sally has been elected president of the class." The calls can be short and still sweet, and especially valued by parents.

The State-of-the-Class Message

Send individual class news notes home. These can be prepared and delivered by students once every month or two. This is a way to keep parents up to date on the activities in each class. Pepper the material with the names of many students.

A Chance to Ask and Suggest

Place a question/suggestion box in an easily accessible place in the classroom, where parents can use it without being seen. They may appreciate this anonymity. Check the box often. Make announcements at meetings to let parents know that their suggestions are given careful thought.

Book and Toy Lending Library

Ask for donations of books, games, and toys from parents and local businesses. Invite parents to check out materials from this library to use at home. Schedule library hours to include at least one after-work hour weekly. Set a limit on the time the materials can be borrowed and stick to it.

Raincoat and Boot Exchange

Set up a day (perhaps tied to an Open House) for children and parents to drop off outgrown items and pick up those from other homes. Raincoats and boots, for example, rarely wear out. This activity saves parents money and brings them into the school. Such an exchange recycles useful clothing and parents really appreciate the service.

Book Swap

Encourage parents and children to do more reading. Ask families to donate books for a swap. Each parent and child is entitled to a new batch of books equal to the number contributed. During the last half hour of the event, make all unclaimed books available to anyone who wants them. It's astonishing how popular reading can be when it's such a bargain.

IF YOU'RE HAVING A MEETING, TRY THESE TIPS

New Meeting Hours

Take advantage of working parents' and teachers' time schedules at the end of a tiring day. Start the meeting at 6 P.M., bring some sandwich makings, and be home at 8:30

instead of 11 P.M. This may spark new membership and avoid the competition between the meeting and TV offerings.

Open House Time

First impressions are often lasting. For many parents, Back-to-School Night may be their first and only contact with the school during the year. Make it a night to remember with a few of the following ideas:

- Have students prepare a special welcome message for parents to display outside the classroom.

- Let students make self-portraits and place them over their desk chairs. Ask parents to find their children's desk by identifying these self-portraits.

- Ask students to make a "mailbox" to attach to the back of the chairs. Friends and parents can leave notes for children to find the morning after Open House.

Have students explain what's happening in the classroom. After a hard day, teachers get a chance to relax, and youngsters get a chance to shine. Parents enjoy it more too.

Family Evening

Think about a family field trip for the whole "school family." See a play or movie together, for example. This opens channels for discussions among children, parents, and teachers. Employed mothers and single parents have found such events a good way to meet other parents. Set up a pool of parent and teacher "buddies" to accompany children whose parents are unable to join the event.

41

We're Glad You're Here

Introduce new parents to your school with a big welcome. Prepare a packet of basic information about the school and the local community. This can include a school handbook, recent school menus, the student newspaper, the PTA newsletter, and general information about the community such as bus schedules, brochures from banks, realtors, and other businesses. Identify parents who want to get involved in the school. Send home a class survey sheet asking parents about their willingness to serve on committees or as volunteers, or to be contacted by another parent.

Positive responses by new parents can be followed up by having a PTA representative call on them at home, take them on a tour of the community, and accompany them to the first PTA meeting.

At-Home Meetings with Neighborhood Parents

Ask a host parent to invite neighbors in to meet the school principal, guidance counselor, or teacher. An informal, at-home meeting helps build nonthreatening school-parent rapport. Ask members of the group to present and share ideas for home learning activities and for child care when parents are away at work.

Solving Children's and Family Problems Together

Plan a grade-level meeting to discuss discipline and child-care concerns. Invite all parents, not just parents of children with problems. At the meeting, try role playing to illustrate children's needs and behaviors. Teachers can play the roles of students and parents can play the roles of teachers and school staff.

Try to draw out solutions from parents and teachers working together. Use feedback forms to assess immediate and longer-term reactions to the session.

Curriculum Workshops for Families

Provide parents with information and material they need to work with their children at home. Emphasize what parents can do at home to keep children constructively busy. The parent who will not attend a general open house may be more likely to attend a workshop on reading, writing, and arithmetic. These are the "payoff" skills—they pay off in higher parent attendance at school meetings.

Remember Child Care

Many families stay home, away from school events, because they have no one to care for their young children. In setting up a meeting, it is strategic to set up a child-care room and to advertise it well in advance. This is a service many parents would be willing to pay for, or perhaps it can be paid for by the PTA. When involving parents in the school, child care can make all the difference in the world.

INFORMATION SHARING—GOOD AT ANY GRADE

Parent Information Center

To serve the entire school (or if at all possible, within each classroom), set up a comfortable sitting area for parents somewhere in the school building. Furnish it with adult-sized chairs, a table, a lamp, a small rug, and a bulletin board. Use this area for parent conferences.

This parent information center does not require much room. Use a shelf for books from the library, or pamphlets to share. Assembling a list of books and materials on parenthood and child resources in the community is a valuable service for busy families.

This is an excellent project for a volunteer or PTA committee. The school newsletter can announce what's available in the "Center."

Community Information for Parents

Share with parents news of community resources they might not ordinarily know about—after-school programs, garage sales, special local outings, new regulations on food stamps or welfare needs, etc. Clip these items from newspapers. For foreign parents, it is helpful to have news translated into their languages, if possible.

PARENT INVOLVEMENT—EVEN IN SECONDARY SCHOOL

The degree of parent involvement usually declines drastically as children reach the teenage years. The major reasons are as follows:

- Teenagers are finding their own identity and asserting their independence of adults. As they look more to their peers for friendship and approval, they resist having mom or dad "hanging around."

- Parents are baffled and frustrated by their adolescents— who are simultaneously grown up and not grown up.

- The structure of secondary education also contributes to the decline of parent involvement. Reaching out to parents is a much easier job with more clear-cut responsibility in the self-contained elementary classrooms when one teacher each year is primarily responsible for connecting with parents. In the secondary grades, that responsibility is spread out among the guidance counselors and a number of subject-matter teachers.

44

Secondary teachers are particularly concerned that somehow parents no longer care. As indicated above, this parent letup is both natural (the student's age) and structural (the organization of instruction often does not encourage parent involvement). A review of the school's approach to parent involvement can clarify specific roles and responsibilities and lead to more systematic practices. For example, it may be possible to designate one of the student's major subject teachers as the liaison to the family. This can provide a sense of personal teacher contact for parents and help to ensure that the teacher and parent connect—even in the secondary grades.

What continues to be clear despite the confusion of the teenage years is that adolescents need adult guidance and support, and parents play a critical role in their adolescents' education. Parents are the primary role models and teachers in making career decisions, and in such areas as values, and developing the functional life skills needed to hold a job and manage a household.

The Leadership Role of the Teacher

What also continues to be clear, despite the more diffused patterns of school-family communication in the secondary grades, is that teachers are in key roles to provide guidance and support to parents in understanding and fulfilling their educational responsibilities to their adolescents. Some school subjects lend themselves more readily to parent involvement activities than others. For example, it is easier to find ways to involve parents in subjects such as health, home economics, or general mathematics than it is in advanced algebra or physics. But each subject matter specialist can probably come up with one or two ways in which parents could be involved in a practical application of the subject area or in an enrich-

45

ment activity. Units in study skills or career exploration offer rich parent involvement opportunities.

One way to start is for each secondary teacher to design one activity each marking period for parent and student to do together. Suggestions in several subject areas follow.

Worlds Enough and Time (Study Skills)

Young people, like their parents, are pulled in many different directions and feel a great deal of pressure in their use of time. Ask the student and parent to keep a record of their time use for a week as an exercise in observation and recording. Parent and student can use this to analyze their use of time: What are the patterns? Where are the problems? Each family should be able to come up with at least two specific recommendations for better time management.

Family Fitness (Health)

Fitness is "in." This can be an activity in which the whole family can join. It could be as simple as a few stretch exercises or jogging, or it could involve attending an aerobic exercise class together. The important thing is to find a convenient time, make the commitment, and keep at it. Teachers can provide information on nearby exercise programs.

Career Exploration (Social Studies)

Ask students to identify one or two jobs that they find interesting and appealing. Ask family members to help students find out more about these jobs—what the work involves, qualifications, salary, and future prospects.

46

Costing Out Wheels (General Math)

Driving is considered the natural birthright of most teenagers, but they need to understand the costs involved in owning and maintaining a car. Ask students to draw up an estimated annual budget for an automobile with the help of their parents. Include monthly payments, registration and insurance, oil and gas, routine maintenance, and an allowance for repairs.

This activity can be extended to other areas, such as the costs involved in maintaining a house or an apartment.

Family Food Shopper (Math or Home Economics)

Encourage families to let teenagers plan the family menu for a week and do the necessary shopping within the confines of a predetermined budget. The teenager will be amazed at how much groceries cost and will have a new respect for mom or dad as a household manager.

Consumer Research (Math)

Let the teenager take the initiative in doing the research for making a planned family purchase of a major item such as a new TV, a microwave, or a new set of tires. The student takes responsibility for gathering the ads, comparing the model features and prices, checking the consumer guides, warranties, manufacturer and dealer reliability, service, etc. Final choices can be presented to the family for discussion and possible purchase.

Family News Analysis (English, Social Studies)

Ask students to watch a news program with their parents and to select one item for family discussion and analysis.

What were the issues involved? Did the coverage seem fair? What is the significance of the event? Encourage students to do this on a weekly basis with their parents.

TV Drama (English)

Have the family discuss one of its favorite sitcoms, soaps, or action series. What do they like about this program? Students can present their family's reactions in a written or oral report.

Understanding and Discipline

Perhaps just as important as involvement with students' academic progress in the secondary grades is the involvement parents show through concern and knowledge about their teenagers' schooling and daily life experience. The activities that follow suggest what every teacher can do to ensure that families are kept informed about these matters.

Mastering the School Schedule

Parents need to know what's coming up in order to guide and monitor their child's use of time, and to plan family events around the school schedule. Schools can help by providing parents with a school calendar. At the beginning of the term, subject area teachers can send home the anticipated dates of reports, major tests, and other key assignments, and these can be penciled in on the calendar. Sports and club activities can also be added. Having all this information in one easy-to-read location is very helpful to both the parent and the student.

Communication About School Policies and Expectations

Information about school policies with regard to attendance, dress, completion of homework, and the discipline code is usually buried in the school handbook. A note to parents at the beginning of each year concerning these policies and expectations is a helpful reminder.

Parent Support Groups

Not all parents can or will attend meetings, but forming parent support groups and facilitating them can be useful to parents who are experiencing difficulty in communicating with their children. A basic concern for many parents is how students deal with the temptations and risks of substance abuse and sex. The school should make clear how these topics are covered in the school curriculum. Meetings can be held so that parents can voice their concerns and so that the roles of the parents and the school can be mutually reinforcing.

Chapter 6
THE PARENT-TEACHER CONFERENCE

A parent-teacher conference is one of the best ways to fulfill the adult needs for information, for reassurance, and for practical advice—especially if it is planned and carried out to ensure clear communication. The goal of the conference is to transform bits of information shared by parent and teacher into integrated knowledge that can be acted upon.

A successful parent-teacher conference is a three-stage process. It includes thinking and action that take place: *before* the conference, *at* the conference, and *after* the conference. It is a real partnership between home and school in all three stages. The *before* and *after* stages can be just as important as the conference itself. The tips that follow focus on these often overlooked yet critically important times.

BEFORE THE CONFERENCE

- Try not to bring memories of previous conferences into this conference.
- Be ready to share your concerns, your problems—without trying to assign blame.
- Focus on the purpose of the conference. Early in the year, it might be to meet one another or to learn more about the child; later in the year, it might be to focus on a particular problem.
- Both parents and teachers should also make a list of questions to ask each other. For example, parents might want to know: What is being taught this year? How does my child get along with other children in class?

How can I help my child at home? Teachers might ask: What does your child do outside school? What differences are there in your child between this year and last? What does your child like or dislike now?

- When sending home notices about the conference schedule, encourage parents to make a list of their concerns and bring it to the conference.

AT THE CONFERENCE

- Encourage parents to consider the following questions. They are stated here from the parents' point of view.
  How is my child progressing?
  How can we help our child at home?
  How well does our child work independently?
  How does our child relate to others in the class?
  Does my child like school?
  What are my child's specific strengths and/or weaknesses?
- Toward the end of the conference, review what has been said and the steps that are planned for followup. This gives both teacher and parents the chance to clear up any misunderstandings that may have taken place.
- Followup on the conference is vital. Tell parents to call, not the next day, but in a few weeks, to see how things are going. Ask them to leave a message as needed for you to call back.

AFTER THE CONFERENCE

- This is an important time for teachers to take stock and to follow up on the suggestions made at the conference. It is important to ask such questions as—
  Was this conference a friendly, useful meeting?

51

What were the parents' reactions?
What did I learn that will help me reach and teach this child?
Did the parents learn more about their child?
Did I learn more about the parents and their needs and their daily lives?
Did the parents leave with a friendly, optimistic attitude?
Did we all emerge with specific, practical ways to help the child?

The checklist that follows, used as a followup reminder, can be helpful to both parents and teachers.

At our recent conference, we agreed to the following:

_____

_____

_____

Please let me know how we are doing (check the answers that apply):

Are the ideas working:

    Consistently? _____   Sometimes? _____   Not at all? _____

Would you like to continue?   Yes _____   No _____

Should we change our plan?   Yes _____   No _____

If so, to what? _____

Is another conference needed?   Yes _____   No _____

    In person? _____   Or by phone? _____

Additional comments?

_____

_____

SUMMARY

A parent should walk away ready to follow one or more of the specific recommendations made during the conference—checking on the child's homework, cutting down TV watching time, getting children to use an alarm clock for wake-up and study times. The list will vary, but it cries out not just for talk—but for ACTION! A well-planned and well-conducted conference, like home learning activities, will move parents to positive action on behalf of their children's education.

Chapter 7
SPECIAL ATTENTION
FOR SINGLE PARENTS

Studies have found that the pain of divorce does have an effect on children's work in school—at least for a while. Teachers are concerned about what do do. The current situation is unique. In many school systems, large numbers of students are living in homes where the parents are separated or divorced. The optimistic news, however, is that schools are more ready than ever before to respond positively to single parents.

This chapter reviews the research on single-parent families, the trauma of divorce, and its effect on children. It also provides information that teachers can share with single-parent families, in order to help these parents carry out their responsibilities for their children's education. For children, the time of divorce is a traumatic period; this fact should not be minimized. Teachers, however, are in a position to be helpful to parents struggling to get through a difficult experience.

THE PAIN OF DIVORCE

At the recent HSI conference on Single-Parent Families and the Schools, the following were among the basic concerns of single parents:

School personnel are insensitive. They stereotype children from single-parent families and expect less from them. Schools do not provide the before- and after-school care that children of working and single parents need. School meetings

54

and parent-teacher conferences are scheduled as if parents do not work and are planned as though there are still fathers in the home. (18)

Parents are asking for better communication between home and school; they are looking for signs that schools and teachers understand how today's families live.

THE SCHOOL'S CONCERN

Is what happens to the family a concern of the school? Not long ago the answer might have been no. Today, however, the educational impact of the family and the home is known. Teachers are now in a unique position to provide help and support to single parents and their children. But this assistance depends on preparing parents to work in partnership with the school, and in many cases, improving the lines of communication.

Teachers need help from parents, which they often do not receive. For example, parents may be reluctant to provide the information schools need in order to help children. In one study, many teachers said that they had suspected a divorce at home but felt it improper and intrusive to inquire (34).

From the parent's perspective, there are continuing concerns about negative comments made by teachers about one-parent families, including the use of the term "broken home," the need for parents to take time off from work for school conferences, and the lack of school information provided to noncustodial parents (18).

RESEARCH FINDINGS
ON CHILDREN'S SCHOOL ACHIEVEMENT

Because the research on the impact of single-parent families on the children's school achievement is recent, it is more suggestive than definitive. A brief summary is presented here so that teachers can review it and use it as appropriate in discussions with single parents. Most importantly, it is offered to help teachers understand some of the problems faced by parents and children in single-parent families.

A review of numerous studies done for the National Institute of Education (NIE) shows that when the socioeconomic status of families is taken into account, the intelligence of children in one- and two-parent households is similar. Aptitude and achievement test scores are lower for those from one-parent homes, however. This same review of studies also shows that children from one-parent homes tend to receive lower grades, display more disruptive behavior in school, and have poorer attendance (15).

Certain single-parent children do better in school than others. Although the adjustment of both sexes was similar at the time of divorce, girls appeared much better adjusted than boys one year later. Yet girls were not treated much differently than boys by their teachers (34). The intellectual functioning and social development of boys is more adversely affected by living in a one-parent home. Many studies suggest that the impact of marital discord and divorce is more pervasive and enduring for boys than for girls (34).

Children who are very young when their parents divorce fare better psychologically than their older siblings. Five years after the marriage breakup, younger children remembered fewer stressful events, while older children tended to suffer continued damaging memories (18).

Certain circumstances in single-parent homes also affect child functioning. Conflict between the ex-spouses after divorce is harmful to children, especially if it spills over into the parent-child relationship (34). Many mother-child relationships deteriorate in the year immediately after divorce, especially those of mothers and sons. By the second year, parenting improves markedly (34).

Furthermore, children in single-parent families are often

expected to assume added responsibilities. These can lead to greater self-sufficiency, but too much independence and responsibility can also make youngsters feel overwhelmed, incompetent, and resentful (21). Support from friends and family—including grandparents—promotes positive self-esteem for children. And positive relations with teachers, peers, and neighbors help lessen the impact of family stress (14).

Despite their extra burdens, single parents talk with teachers as frequently as do other parents (13). Children from one- and two-parent backgrounds are equally likely to have parents spend time with them on schoolwork. Across white, Black, and Hispanic families, over three-fourths of all mothers are judged to be moderately or highly involved in the education of their children (10).

In short, this research review reveals a solid body of parent interest, caring, and concern that teachers can draw upon and mobilize on behalf of children. Teachers can do this by providing parents with practical information on how to help their children learn.

ADVICE FOR SINGLE PARENTS FROM TEACHERS

The following pages provide supportive, nonintrusive advice that teachers may find useful to share with single parents at conferences and in written communications.

Organize Homelife

In case of divorce, it is advisable to tell children why you are separating as plainly—and with as little bitterness—as possible. Do this together before one spouse leaves, if possible. Give the children enough time to prepare, but not so much that they begin to believe the divorce won't happen.

Organize daily homelife and routines so that they are as constant and continuing as possible. Try to provide the child with a sense of stability in this unstable time.

- Be as specific about the future as you can. Tell children where they will live, where their other parent will live, and how visits will be arranged.
- Follow certain basic rules. Maintain authority. Let children know that you and your spouse will continue their regular routines. For example, bedtimes and chores will remain the same and will be enforced by both parents.

Inform the School

Certain information is helpful and, in fact, necessary to the school. For example:

- Notify the school office of changes in marital status. Ask that the child's report cards and records be sent also to the noncustodial parent. Let the school know of any changes in address, telephone number, or job so that you may always be reached. Be sure this information is complete.
- Set up a conference with the teacher. At this time, try to be as honest as you can about what is happening to the family. Don't predict terrible behavior you expect your child to develop. Let teachers know you will work closely with them to solve any problems.

Ask for the School's Help

Suggest that the school hold meetings so that single, working parents can attend. Find out if child care can be provided at parent meetings. For example, a local high school's family-life class could set up a babysitting room while parents attend school functions.

Connect with the Community

Feeling overwhelmed and alone is one of the first obstacles recent single parents and their children must deal with. The hardest part can be getting started. Try inviting a neighbor to lunch. Meet older neighbors through your citizens association, your church or temple, or your local senior citizens group. Many are ready to provide child care on a regular basis or to help out in an emergency on days when school is canceled but parents are expected at work. Reciprocate by offering to run an errand for them.

Contact the local chapter of Parents Without Partners. This group now has more than 1,000 chapters across the country. Many offer a neighborhood help exchange for household maintenance, babysitting, and scholarships. For more information, check your local telephone directory, or write to Parents Without Partners, 8807 Colesville Road, Silver Spring, MD 20910.

Use the School as a Meeting Place

Use the school as a community resource center. Encourage the PTA to set up programs that are useful for single and working parents on topics such as meeting the demands of home and job life. Ask the principal about organizing support groups for single parents. Such groups may be led by a school counselor and meet in the evenings. The PTA can help get things rolling.

Ask to use the school facilities. Families can band together and set up their own activities. Once a week, the group can plan a potluck supper with everyone bringing a dish. Movies can follow dinner. Also plan regular family outings such as roller skating and hiking. On weekends, members can take turns sitting for children in the group.

Involve Children in Community Activities

Help children organize a picnic or a softball game. Older children can fry chicken; younger ones can help with potato salad or a cake. First and second graders especially like decorating the cake with sprinkles, candy hearts, and tubes of icing.

Joining together with others is rewarding not only to parents, but also to children. As one mother commented: "Going to these events has made it easier for my kids. They see other kids ·at these family activities, and they're going through the same things, and they're surviving and having fun, so it looks like we will, too."

IT CAN BE DONE!

Teachers play a significant leadership role in helping families move through difficult times. The school is a constant, a source of continuing support in a changing world. Teachers need not change the world in order to make positive changes in the lives of many families. Figuring out ways to hold school events at times and places so that single, employed parents can attend is a big step. Providing parents with a list of community resources to help connect adults to community networks is another. This list can include information about before- and after-school care, single-parent clubs, adult education programs, and mental health referral agencies.

Teachers can also help by checking out their own personal assumptions about single parents and by simply avoiding the use of expressions such as "broken home." Teachers need to know the laws relating to single parents, including parental rights regarding report cards. Understanding that children's troubles will be temporary, and that parent support is valuable and needed can be vital contributions of the parent-teacher relationship.

Chapter 8

SCHOOLS AND FAMILIES:
A TIME OF HOPE

To a great extent, teachers today want to help families, but knowing what to do is not easy. The suggestions that follow, which serve as a brief summary of this monograph, provide initial approaches that can be carried out easily without waiting for funding or governmental mandates. Teachers have every reason—including data from research and the experience of common sense—to believe in and follow these four basic rules for involvement programs:

1. Link parents' involvement directly to the learning of their own children. An important reward for parents is their children's school success.

2. Provide ways for families to reinforce academic skills at home. Easy home learning techniques foster learning. For example, young children use the TV schedule to keep to time limits, they dial and read telephone numbers; older students make "best buy" purchases at the grocery store, they use maps to plan family trips.

3. Link the school's work to the community. Teachers must share the responsibility of education. Home learning activities can be distributed at workplaces, churches and temples, gas stations, and grocery stores. They can be adapted for bilingual and special education students. The wider public, including senior citizens, needs to help.

4. Provide for parent involvement at all levels of schooling. Research and parent programs have primarily centered on the early grades, but continuing support is needed as children move through school. Teens need help from home to get the best from the secondary years.

Families and teachers might wish that the school could do the job alone. But today's school needs families and today's families need the school. In many ways, this mutual need may be the greatest hope for change.

APPENDIXES

APPENDIX A. HOME-BASED PARENT INVOLVEMENT

PARENT INVOLVEMENT STRATEGIES: A NEW EMPHASIS ON TRADITIONAL PARENT ROLES*

by Adriana de Kanter and Alan L. Ginsburg, U.S. Department of Education, and Ann M. Milne, Decision Resources Corporation

INTRODUCTION

Research has consistently shown family background to be among the most important influences predicting a child's performance in school (Coleman et al. 1966; Jencks et al. 1972; Mosteller and Moynihan 1972). More recent studies have begun to identify the family attitudes and behaviors that mediate these effects (Walberg 1984; Hanson and Ginsburg 1985; Etzioni 1984). Yet despite the increased knowledge about the importance of the home environment, only a few examples exist of intervention strategies that have succeeded in altering this environment in ways that promote a child's educational development.

This paper proposes a new emphasis on home-based parental involvement, one that takes a realistic approach to the roles accessible to parents of low-achieving children, given potential limitations on their skills and time. This approach is based on encouraging parents to use everyday activities in the home to develop in their children behavior and attitudes that promote academic achievement in school. These approaches are available to, and have been effectively used by, all types of parents. This approach differs from that endorsed in past legislation for parents of Title I children.

The Title I program targeted supplemental services on educationally low performers who resided in low income areas, in part because these children were considered less likely to have the same

*Reprinted with permission from *Designs for Compensatory Education: Conference Proceedings and Papers*, edited by Barbara I. Williams, Peggy A. Richmond, and Beverly J. Mason (Washington, D.C.: Research and Evaluation Associates, Inc., 1986).

educational opportunities at home as other children. This deficit model of the home reflects the origins of the compensatory education program during the "War on Poverty" period in the mid-1960s. Now known as Chapter I of the Education Consolidation and Improvement Act of 1981, the program retains its original purpose.

While Title I largely ignored the natural role of parents as their children's mentor and guardian in the home, it stressed a major role for parents in the school. This school role was more the result of evolving events than of particular provisions in the original legislation. Indeed, the 1965 legislation that spawned Title I simply required parents to generally be "involved" in developing local project applications.

Initial evaluations of learning gains of compensatory education participants were quite disappointing. However, investigations by the NAACP Legal Defense and Education Fund (1969) found that recipient schools and districts so abused the use of compensatory education funds that in many cases no real compensatory education program could be identified. It was reported, instead, that Federal money flowed for peripheral expenditures such as band uniforms, swimming pools, carpeting principals' offices and building construction.

The extensive abuses of legislative intent led to tighter Federal legislation and regulations that included expanded parental oversight. In 1971, Parent Advisory Councils (PACs) were legislated at the district level. In 1974, the law was changed to require councils at the school level as well, with members of all councils to be selected by parents. Then, in 1978, the legislation specified that ". . . each local educational agency shall give each advisory council which it establishes . . . responsibility for advising it, in planning for, and implementation and evaluation of its programs and projects assisted under this title." Section 125(b), (P.L. 95–561).

Parental oversight, however, was not limited to ensuring only that compensatory services reached the intended beneficiaries. It also meant that some parent groups were given oversight approval of the curriculum and the budget itself. In 1979, the Systems Development Corporation (Melaragno, et al. 1981) found that 60 percent of the district-level committees reviewed or signed off on all or part of the budget.

As parent committees became established, funds were also set aside to pay parents for their time and to finance expenses and trips for parent group meetings. The 1976 study of Title I by the National Institute of Education (NIE) identified assistance to parent groups as the largest single support service expense, outweighing expenses for food, nutrition, health, or counseling.

Along with the growth of PACs, the use of parents as aides in the classroom emerged as another type of school-based parent activity. In 1980, case studies at 16 school districts conducting Title I projects revealed that parent aides were found at 75 percent of the sites (Melaragno, et al. 1981).

The duties fulfilled by the parent aides indicated that the most prevalent activities were directly associated with instruction. However, it is not clear that parents of Title I students are most equipped to handle this type of teaching assignment in the school.

The education amendments of 1981 brought about a change in Federal requirements that eliminated the need for local school systems to establish formal advisory councils. This elimination came about as part of general Federal efforts across a number of social programs to return more control over program decisions to local officials. More recently new Department of Education regulations represent a clarification of policies toward parent involvement. Although these regulations list PACs and other school-based strategies as permissible parent activities, the regulations stress a more traditional home-based role for parents.

While there is a legitimate role for school-based activities involving parents, particularly in monitoring compliance with Federal regulations, there are also inherent problems. First, the formation of PACs for a multiplicity of Federal categorical programs, including Chapter I, is excessively burdensome to school officials. The schools' and districts' solicitation of parental involvement is, at first, time-consuming and then administratively awkward and complex. Even if PACs are successfully begun, the results of parent participation in PACs are not overwhelming. According to the Sustaining Effects Study, only 14 percent of parents in Title I schools were PAC members (Hinckley 1979).

Second, Federal requirements for the involvement of PACs in

program governance activities such as project planning, implementation, and evaluation place low-income parents in an awkward position. While they may be able to judge whether or not their children are learning in school, they may have difficulty making decisions on specific issues of school operations, such as assessing the adequacy of curriculum. Yet the legislated purpose of PACs is for this type of involvement.

The use of low-income parents as Chapter I aides is also problematic. These parents, who are most likely to have little or no higher education, are being used for instructional purposes. In 1976, it was found that 24 percent of compensatory education was provided by paraprofessionals, compared with only 4 percent of regular instruction (NIE 1977). In essence, disadvantaged children are being exposed to teachers with far less education than children in the mainstream curriculum. Yet, disadvantaged children are exactly those students who most need professional attention.

Finally, the formation of PACs for parents of disadvantaged children is segregative. While compensatory students spend no more than one-fifth of their school day in Chapter I activities, by forming a PAC their parents deal only with this fragment of their education and remain isolated from the goings-on of the total school program. Indeed, Chapter I parents remain insulated from the major parent-school groups, such as the PTA, who are concerned with overall educational quality. Only through parental participation in groups concerned with whole-school progress will the needs of disadvantaged children be met.

This paper examines parental involvement strategies that emphasize traditional home-based activities. Since the environment of low- and high-achieving students often differs in ways that are important for assessing home-based strategies, we begin with a description of the characteristics of low achievers over which parents can exert influence and which research shows can affect student achievement.

CHARACTERISTICS OF LOW ACHIEVERS
OVER WHICH PARENTS CAN EXERT INFLUENCE

There are many reasons why a student fails to learn in school.

Some may have to do with a student's innate abilities. Others may have to do with school inputs, such as the quality of teachers, class size, or course content. On the other hand, some causes of lower student performance are related to characteristics over which parents could exert control. As Iverson and Walberg (1982) note, academic ability and achievement are more closely linked to the measures of some process and intellectual stimulation variables than to parental socioeconomic status indicators, and the process variables are "changeable and . . . merit constructive efforts to improve them . . ." (p. 151).

These characteristics over which parents could have some influence and which are effective in promoting learning are the ones that we seek to identify in this section so as to point the way for recommendations on appropriate parental involvement efforts. Four characteristics are considered: student values, behavior in school, use of time, and access to educational resources outside the school.

Student Values

Students' values determine what youngsters believe is important in their life. Hence, values establish priorities and direct student energies. Students who have priorities that emphasize success in school will expend the effort required to learn. For others who focus on more immediate pleasures, school work may take a backseat to other activities. Values are learned and students tend to assume the values of those close to them; hence, parents and friends have much to do with shaping their values orientation.

A recent study (Hanson and Ginsburg 1985) underscored the importance of traditional values as a predictor of academic achievement. It identified student, parent, and peer values to be important predictors for academic success. Students' values included belief in the work ethic, taking responsibility for one's own actions, and religious values. Parents' values focused on their general level of encouragement and concern, attributes which encourage responsible behavior in their children. Peers' values emphasized the importance they attached to education, and thus, reinforce a student's own efforts to succeed in school.

69

Examining 15,000 high school sophomores, this study found that these traditional values, as predictors of academic success as measured by a standardized achievement test, were twice as important as family economic or educational background. Moreover, the greater relative importance of value characteristics held up when the outcome measure was changed to grades in school or to educational improvement between the sophomore and senior years.

Mayeske's (1973) extensive reanalysis of the Coleman report identified three motivational variables as playing a key role in student achievement. These were student and parent educational expectations of students, attitudes toward hard work and responsibility as antecedents of success, and participation in educational supportive activities in the home. Also, parental encouragement for education has been shown by Sewell and Hauser (1972) to have a "net value" of six-tenths of a year of higher education when other factors are controlled. These authors note the importance for higher education attainment of peer expectations, or having friends who plan on attending college.

Freeman (1985) has found that another value variable—religiosity—is important in affecting the extent to which disadvantaged ghetto youths hold a job when they leave school. He notes that religiosity is not just an indicator of who are "good kids," but that at least some part of the impact is causal.

Recent evidence of the influence which traditional values can exert to enable students to overcome barriers to success is offered in a study of Asian refugees to this country (Caplan 1985). These families came to this country often with few material possessions, little formal education, and not knowing the English language. Investigation of the correlates of their accomplishments attributed much of the academic success of the refugee children to family values brought from Indochina. The three values rated as most important by 95 percent of the Indochinese families were educational achievement, a cohesive family, and a belief in hard work. The author concludes that "these data suggest that cultural values and family-centered achievement orientations and strategies can determine high levels of educational achievement, even where income and formal education resources are minimal" (p. 50).

70

Bloom's (1985) study of the most gifted and talented students in our society confirms the importance of parental reinforcement of students' efforts as a factor for even our best students to succeed. Bloom observed that many of the most successful students were not possessed with unique brillance. Rather, what distinguished them from others was an enormous drive for success and perfection. The author cites parental support as a major source of this drive. Other research (Weiner 1973) suggests that even for less able students, extra effort can overcome the handicap of low ability.

The importance of values orientation as a predictor of educational success is particularly significant for participants in compensatory education. These are the kinds of characteristics over which all parents, regardless of their education or income, could exert control.

Behavior in School

Students' behavior affects achievement, and is, in turn, affected by parental input. Students who fail to follow instructions, frequently interrupt class, or are in trouble with the law are not likely to possess the self-discipline to meet academic challenges. Recent research supports the link between poor discipline and low academic performance.

Low-achieving (i.e., lowest quartile) high school sophomores are 60 percent more likely to cut class compared with high achievers, 25 percent more likely to be viewed by their friends as troublemakers, and 20 percent more likely to be in trouble with the law.

A study by Myers et al. (1985) demonstrated that misbehavior among sophomore students had negative effects on their grades as sophomores. Further, misbehavior affected the learning that occurred between sophomore and senior years; this is an important finding in demonstrating that student misbehavior is causally connected to lower achievement. In case studies of low-achieving poor ghetto children, Clark (1983) observed that "rules for household conduct, when they exist, tend to be nebulous and contradictory or sporadically enforced" (p. 194).

Lack of discipline has consequences that are not limited to the problem student. Learning does not effectively take place in a

71

climate of fear or when there are frequent classroom disruptions. Moreover, it is the disadvantaged student who is the most likely victim. For example, Blacks and Hispanics were more than twice as likely as whites to be the victims of serious assaults at school (NIE 1978). Equal opportunity for minorities should include the right to attend orderly schools.

Thus, parents and students have good reason in judging school discipline as a major problem confronting our schools. In 16 of the last 17 Gallup Opinion Polls (Gallup 1985), parents ranked lack of school discipline as their number one problem. When Goodlad (1982) surveyed junior and senior high school students as to their "one biggest problem," student misbehavior was listed number one by junior high school students, and alcohol and drug use—a related problem—was rated first by high school seniors.

Research has connected a student's lack of discipline problems with the values described above, and with parents' influence on these values. Hanson and Ginsburg (1985) found that students are less likely to be a discipline problem if they hold positive values related to personal responsibility, religion, and high educational expectations, if their parents are concerned and monitor their behavior, and if they choose friends who value education. Thus, promoting positive values in children is also an important strategy for controlling misbehavior.

It is a strategy open to all parents. Earlier researchers (e.g., Chloward and Ohlin 1960) suggested that the poor socialization and academic deficiencies brought to school by lower-class students made them more prone to fail in school and then to become behavior problems. Later research (Polk and Halferty 1966) found surprisingly little class difference in the backgrounds of delinquents and nondelinquents. Coleman (et al. 1982) notes that "the family structure and authority has clearly weakened in recent years . . . there appears to be a reduced interest on the part of parents in regarding their adolescent children as full members of their family subject to their attention and authority, and a reduced willingness on the part of adolescents to being subject to family constraints and obligations" (p. 190). Parents can take active measures to reverse this trend.

72

Students' Use of Their Out-of-School Time

One of the robust findings of the school effectiveness literature is that the amount learned is related to the time classrooms devote to instruction and that substantial differences in learning time take place among schools and classrooms. Analogously, the amount students learn can be related to their effective use of time out of school.

As early as 1967, Rankin found when comparing high-achieving students and low-achieving students that particular parental behaviors at home and in connection with the school differ significantly between these groups. Parents of high-achieving students initiate more contact with their children's school, provide a wide variety of experiences for their children, and engage in activities encouraging achievement such as helping with homework and talking about school. These characteristics of successful families have been documented by others (Smith 1968; Clark 1984; Walberg 1984) in both single- and two-parent homes and in poor and middle-class families whose children do well in school.

It seems likely that parents can help their children's academic success through exercising control over their leisure time by curbing television viewing and encouraging homework, reading, and conversation.

Television

Television viewing is not necessarily detrimental to learning. Younger children learn vocabulary and, depending on the programs watched, students can learn about the surrounding world. Problems occur when television watching becomes excessive so that television becomes the primary source of out-of-school knowledge and interferes with more productive uses of time. In view of this, it is disturbing that the National Assessment of Educational Progress (NAEP) (Department of Education 1985) found that a full quarter of nine-year-olds watched more than six hours of television per day. In general, television viewing in excess of two hours a day is considered detrimental to school performance. Data from the Sustaining Effects Survey (SES) of 12,000 nationally representative elementary school students, grades 1 through 6, demonstrate that elementary school children who watched four or more hours of TV per day had an 80 percent greater chance of falling into the lowest rather than the highest quartile of reading achievement.

Television fosters a learning process built around rapid but brief presentations of information rather than sustained concentration on material required for an in-depth understanding of topics. At the preschool level, Elkind (1986) suggests that "the rapid presentation of material" on programs such as "Sesame Street" and the "Electric Company" is much too fast for the information processing abilities of young children. These programs, he proposes, "have amplified the attention limitations of young children," with negative consequences for their reading abilities in later life. Similarly, Postman (1986) observes that TV, with its emphasis on visual scenes to provide information with frequent commercial interruptions, discourages development of sustained and critical thinking skills.

Reading

Reading is basic to all learning. It is also a subject that is easily practiced at home. The Department of Education's recent report, *Becoming a Nation of Readers* (1985), emphasized the importance of leisure reading. For example, their study of fifth graders found that 50 percent read books for an average of only four minutes a day, but devoted 130 minutes to viewing television. Reading at home works to improve reading achievement scores. To illustrate, an analysis of 12,000 nationally representative elementary school students in the SES study (Milne et al. in press) estimated that an hour of reading at home each day would increase reading achievement scores by about one-fifth standard deviation (up to 6 percentile points), after controlling for family structure and economic and educational variables.

Becoming a Nation of Readers speaks directly to children and parents recommending that:

- *Children should spend more time in independent reading.* Independent reading, whether in school or out of school, is associated with gains in reading achievement. By the time they are in the third or fourth grade, children should read independently a minimum of two hours per week. Children's reading should include classic and modern works of fiction and nonfiction that represent the core of our cultural heritage.

- *Parents should support school-aged children's continued growth as readers.* Parents of children who become successful readers monitor their children's progress in school . . . buy their children books or take them to libraries, encourage reading as a free time activity, and place reasonable limits on such activities as TV viewing.

Hewison and Tizard (1980) found that children of working-class parents who listened to their children read at home had significantly higher reading performance at ages seven and eight than children whose parents did not listen to them read. Following up on this research, Tizard et al. (1982) found significantly greater gains in reading performance for children ages six and seven whose parents listened to them read at home daily compared with a group receiving extra tutoring in school and with a noninterventional control group. This effect was observed for all ability levels of reading.

Homework

Homework provides students with extra studying. The U.S. Education Department's *What Works* (1986) concludes that when low-ability students do one to three hours of homework a week, their grades are usually as high as those of average-ability students who do not do homework. Similarly, when average-ability students do three to five hours of homework, their grades usually equal those of high-ability students who do no homework. Further, Walberg (1984) estimates that homework that is graded and commented upon can have three times the effect that socioeconomic status has on learning. Homework that is merely assigned can have an effect on learning comparable to socioeconomic status.

However, time spent doing homework is a complex variable to understand. First, simply giving students homework is not nearly as valuable as when it is accompanied by feedback from the teacher (Walberg 1984). Also, less able students may spend more time doing homework because they have greater difficulty doing the assignment.

75

Conversing

Parents taking an interest in their child's activities and talking about them seems to be an important factor in enhancing student achievement for both high and low achievers. Indeed, research focusing on National Merit Scholars showed they all shared only one common characteristic—almost every evening at dinner with their parents, they discussed world events. Clark's (1983) study of low achievers' homes observed that parents found time for television, "but seldom hold family dialogues, except during arguments" (p. 195).

Building on the findings of *Becoming a Nation of Readers* (1985), *What Works* (1986) ties reading with conversing. "Reading instruction builds on conversational skills. To succeed at reading, children need a basic vocabulary, some knowledge of the world around them, and the ability to talk about what they know. Conversing with children about the world around them will help them reflect on past experiences and on what they will see, do, and read about in the future" (p. 15).

It appears that such family routines as regularly scheduled meals provide opportunities for family interactions and discussions that promote learning. Benson et al. (1980) note that family members eating together seems to enhance achievement for students from low socioeconomic status families.

Resources That Can Promote Education

One of the deficits historically perceived as being associated with need for compensatory services is a lack of resources in the home. These resources include both human and material inputs that could promote learning. While some resources may not be available to families of compensatory education students, research has shown that academic achievement is related to other resources that are available to all families.

Books in the Home

A number of studies have shown the importance to achievement of having books and other reading materials in the home. The

"Reading Report Card" (NIE 1985) notes that "relationships between available reading materials and reading proficiency are as notable as those for level of parental education." (p. 50). Other studies (e.g., Milne et al. in press) have shown that, for nationally representative samples of elementary and high school students, reading and mathematics achievement are both related to the number of books in the home. For example, an elementary student in whose home there are no books at his/her reading level is 15 times more likely to be in the lowest quartile than in the highest-achieving quartile; conversely, a child with 50 or more such books is five times more likely to be in the highest-achieving than in the lowest-achieving quartile.

Libraries and Museums

Access to libraries and museums can also support achievement. As Heyns (1978) found, both proximity to, and regular use of, a library were correlates of summer learning or achievement. Both variables were to some extent proxies for number of books read or time spent reading (and effects therefore diminished when such controls were exercised). However, Heyns found distance to library from home related to number of books read, thus indicating that access to a library exerts an independent influence over reading. Thus, while we have no information on the tradeoffs between books in the home, and books from the library, both clearly can contribute to achievement.

Benson et al. (1980) also note that family visits to area cultural centers (museums, aquariums, etc.) are correlated with achievement across sixth graders. However, the achievement of lower income children did not benefit from such visits.

A Place to Study

The high achievement of Japanese children has been largely attributed to their parents' intervention in stimulating and encouraging the child to learn at home (Sava 1985). One of the most important practices of Japanese parents is to create a learning atmosphere. For example, home-study desks are purchased when children are very young (three to five years old). All models of these desks have a high front and sides that minimize distractions. There is a built-in study light, shelves, a clock, electric pencil sharpener, and calculator.

Studies in the United States have recognized the importance of providing children with a place to study. Smith (1968) reports greater achievement gains among elementary school children whose parents employed methods such as providing a time and place at home for the completion of homework.

Parents as Educational Resources

The usefulness of parents as educational resources for their children depends in part on parent attributes and characteristics, not all of which are subject to manipulation nor available to parents of disadvantaged students. It is for this reason that we suggest that, for this target group, parent activities in direct educational instruction with their children should not be emphasized as the sole or even primary method of parental involvement.

There is a wealth of literature on the relationship between family socioeconomic status—particularly income and education—and student achievement (e.g., Coleman et al. 1966; Jencks et al. 1972). The recent challenge for researchers has been to determine how these effects are mediated—through which parental actions on family processes the effect takes place. In particular, authors dealing with human capital development (e.g., Leibowitz 1974, 1977; Goldberg 1977) point out that there are a number of mechanisms through which these family demographic variables affect educational outcomes. One is inheritance of intellectual ability, not a manipulable characteristic. A second may be the absence of a father, which reduces material and human resource availability. A third is through the greater efficiency of the better educated mother as a teacher of her children (Goldberg 1977), affected in part by the fact that mothers spend four times as much time with children as do fathers (Leibowitz 1974). These are all mechanisms which would appear to be primarily available to parents of higher socioeconomic status.

However, as many authors have noted (Walberg 1984, 1981; Bradley and Caldwell 1977; Hanson and Ginsburg 1985) these

78

family socioeconomic and structure variables can often be shown to account for less of the variance in school achievement than family process or environment variables. Henderson (1981) cites the various reanalyses of the Coleman data as supporting a "subtle but compelling argument for parent involvement." Less subtle and more compelling are the numerous studies cited in previous sections of this paper supporting the fact that there are behaviors available to all parents that can make meaningful contributions to educational achievement. These behaviors involve parents' time use, parents' monitoring of their children's time use, and parental inculcation of values.

HOW THE SCHOOL CAN HELP

What used to be considered as basic obligations that parents had to fulfill in order for their child to develop and be educated—the teaching of values, respect for authority, etc.—can no longer be taken for granted. As James Coleman noted in his 1985 Ryerson lecture at the University of Chicago, "Traditionally, the school has needed the support and sustenance provided by the family, in its task of educating children. Increasingly, the family itself needs support and sustenance from the school—and through the school, from the other families with children in the school—in its task of raising children."

The underlying reasons for the weakening of family support mechanisms are fairly apparent. First, Coleman has suggested that parents have less self-interest in investing the personal time and financial resources to promote their children's development. Children are less important as both parents have become more career oriented, work longer before having a family, and are less dependent upon children for financial support after retirement. Second, the rise in one-parent families and the related increase in proportion of children from families in poverty mean fewer home resources to invest in children. Third, the dominance of television as a leisure pasttime has eroded traditional parent-child contact through conversation and other family activities. While parents remain their child's first and primary educator, this role has largely been ignored by professional educators.

Coleman (1985), who recognizes this problem, proposes to "use the schools to strengthen the family's capacity to raise its children; in the ghetto and the suburbs, it implies active involvement of the school in helping to strengthen the norms that parents hold for their children . . ." (p. 22) Schools should also take initiatives to help parents support their child's educational development at home.

The schools have been quick to blame parents for failure; U.S. teachers say the biggest problem facing the schools is "parent lack of interest and support" (Gallup 1984). Nevertheless, the schools have not done their part to reach out and help those parents who want to become involved. Dorothy Rich (1985), based on her extensive experience in home-school development programs, describes what she terms "a teacher's pitfall." The common complaints from parents are: "Teachers don't listen to us." "They feel we have nothing to offer." "They don't respect us." (p. 14). In essence, teachers and school officials will need prodding and help if parent involvement is to be successful.

This section considers what schools and communities could do to foster a realistic approach to parent involvement.

Teaching Values

Today, the teaching of fundamental values—honesty, integrity, responsibility, and the work ethic—in the public schools is controversial. Foes argue that in our modern technological and pluralistic society, the idea that absolute standards of conduct can guide behavior is an anachronism. They believe that the only supportable curriculum in today's modern world seems to be a value-free curriculum. The aim of this educational philosophy is to adapt to the different viewpoints embedded in our pluralistic society by creating a pedagogy in which all values are personal and relative.

This approach is not succeeding in its lofty aims of improving our understanding of and ability to deal with complex social issues. The basic premises on which it is built are flawed—that education should be value-free; that students are able to evolve their own concepts of right and wrong without adult guidance; that a value-free education is unbiased in its presentation of issues; and, that this form of instruction promotes higher-order thinking and reasoning.

The stark truth is that the transmission of cultural values by our schools has historically characterized American education. From the nineteenth century *McGuffey's Readers* to the 1948 NEA handbook, children have been taught to read and write through poems and rhymes, riddles and essays that stress personal and civic virtues. As Honig (1985) noted in his recent book *Last Chance for Our Children*,". . . these texts were on to something—the power of stories to edify as they entertain . . ." (p. 10).

The public schools can provide that help again. As Honig noted, "Indeed, that may be their unique and essential purpose in the United States—to bind together a diverse and pluralistic society by disseminating the guiding morality that inheres in our best literature and history" (p. 107).

Recent surveys indicate that the American public recognizes that the teaching of fundamental American values belongs as an integral part of a normal education curriculum. When questioned by the Sixteenth Annual Gallup Poll (1984) of the Public's Attitudes Toward the Public Schools on the goal of education, the highest rated response next to "speaking and writing correctly," was "to develop standards of what is 'right' and 'wrong'." An earlier Gallup Poll (1983) revealed that 79 percent of Americans favor public school instruction that deals with ethical and moral behavior; among parents of public school students, 84 percent favored the teaching of values in their children's schools.

The schools need to respond to this imperative. They need to bring a message to their students that is consistent with the values they learn in the home—respect for authority, the virtue of hard work, and the worth of self-discipline.

And this does not mean that schools need to create a course entitled "Values Education." Rather, schools must teach in the classroom values through stories and studies in history, literature, and civics. Schools can undertake policies, such as that recently adopted by the California system, to teach the classics. There the ideals of civilization can best be illustrated.

81

What's Expected of Students

Along with teaching students about the importance of basic values related to standards of conduct or ideals, schools must put these values into practice. Students must know what's expected of them and they must be held responsible for their behavior. Moreover, parents need to know what schools expect of their children so that they can reinforce these expectations at home.

Codes of school conduct are not a novel idea, but they have in recent years become more of a legal document to protect a school system and its employees against law suits instead of a simple statement of the school's expectations for its students. For example, the Boston Safe Schools Commission (1983), established to reduce high rates of violence and disruption, concluded "there must be a greater clarity in Boston about what behavior is expected. The intent of the present Code of Discipline has not been well enough understood or communicated, in large part because it is too lengthy and technical in its language" (p. 17).

In addition, codes of school conduct should be comprehensive in scope and cover expectations regarding academic as well as disciplinary conduct. It's not sufficient that a student simply show up at school and not cause trouble to pass. Students and their parents need to know that they are expected to work hard at their academics. Past pressures for social promotions in schools have discouraged clear communication of academic expectations.

An acceptable statement of a school's expectations for its students should, therefore, have at least the following four characteristics: (1) clear statements of what is expected written in simple but specific language; (2) rules of conduct covering such behaviors as attendance, classroom conduct, drug use, and assaults and thefts; (3) expected academic conduct covering such activities as average amount of homework, completion of assignments, and amount of outside reading; (4) definite and consistently enforced penalties for misconduct.

A statement of expectations for students is of little help to parents if they are unaware of such statements. Unfortunately, studies show that a majority of parents are unaware of the nature of such statements. Schools not only must make efforts to ensure that parents receive statements about school policies, but that these statements are read. Some schools, such as those in Buffalo, New York, have had greater success in achieving parental awareness through requiring students to return a signed parental pledge that they, as parents, will reinforce at home, the schools' expectations for student academic and discipline behavior.

What's Expected of Parents

Home-based parent involvement strategies must be realistic in what they set out to accomplish. They should establish a set of roles that a responsible parent will carry out. These are responsibilities that focus on attitudes and behaviors. Some potentially worthy activities, especially those involving direct parent-child instruction, are simply not ones that we could expect most parents to undertake. Too few parents are willing or have the time required and, beyond the early elementary grades, many parents may not have the knowledge.

We previously identified a list of parent responsibilities in the home that we propose schools emphasize. They are supported by research and are akin to the activities that parents would normally carry out in fulfilling their duties as their child's guardian. Examples included instilling children with a sense of worth and importance of accomplishment, promoting good discipline, and monitoring the child's use of time.

Schools can provide specific guidance as to what parents should do in each area through four types of strategies. One is to establish a set of *specific everyday activities* for parents to do to reinforce their children's learning. The list would include ensuring completion of homework, conversing about school activities, limiting a child's television viewing, or encouraging the reading of books, activities which all parents can manage and which research has demonstrated proves effective. Having parents sign homework and keep a daily checklist on their accomplishments in other activity areas represents a simple mechanism by which many schools foster home-based involvement.

The Jacksonville school district implements an "everyday" activi-

83

ties strategy. At the beginning of the school year a "back-to-school-night" is hosted by the district. Parents are given an orientation where they are told of their responsibilities and where they receive a year-long calendar marked with major school and district events. In addition to these events, the district marks suggested activities to do with your child. The calendar is grade-specific, based on the age of the parent's child, and the activities are coordinated with the curriculum. For example, if the child is studying nutrition, then the parent is encouraged to take the child to the grocery store to study nutritional labels on the groceries.

Parents will also need *encouragement to get involved*. Many parents, especially those who lack substantial schooling, may find the school a frightening place. Others haven't realized the importance. Honig (1985) reports on some Oakland public schools that increased attendance at parents' back-to-school night primarily by running "parent participation programs like a political campaign. In English class, students wrote invitations to parents asking them to attend. Teachers manned the contests. Contests were held pitting one class against another, with each one having the highest parental attendance rate earning ice cream sundaes" (p. 168). The result was that parent attendance at back-to-school night increased from 15 to 45 percent. To boost attendance at parent-teacher conferences, volunteer parents called up those who initially failed to attend. Attendance jumped to 65 percent. To maintain lines of communication, teachers sent home weekly progress reports with their children's work that parents had to sign.

Parents may also need *help*. Teacher homework hotlines (Fairfax County, Virginia; Indianapolis, Indiana) in which teachers are available to answer phone questions respond to an immediate need for information. However, a more basic and continuing need for assistance is suggested in Joyce Epstein's surveys of first, third, and fifth grade parents and teachers in Maryland school districts. Four-fifths of the parents said that they could spend more time "helping their children at home if they were shown how to do specific learning activities." Further, the study showed that teachers can be effective. Parents of students whose teachers emphasized parent involvement were more likely to feel they should help their children and to receive most of their ideas for home involvement from teachers. Dorothy Rich has developed and successfully tested an extensive set of ideas to assist parents in helping their children at home through everyday activities.

While parent contact with the school is too often associated with negative experiences—your child is in trouble, please come to school—parents must *accept their share of responsibility for their children's improper conduct* or failure to otherwise meet their obligations. Some districts are requiring parent attendance at school as a condition for reinstatement from expulsion. In the case of controlling student drug use, Anne Arundel County (Maryland) has found remarkably effective a policy that requires parents to come to school to cosign an antidrug use pledge with their child and to coparticipate in a drug counseling program.

CONCLUSIONS

While the role of the Federal government in parental involvement has changed, over the years policymakers have not backed away from their belief in the importance of parents in educating their children. Secretary Bennett has made parental involvement one of his major priorities, and the Department of Education is providing leadership, supporting research, disseminating findings, and working through such Federal programs as Chapter 1 and Title VII by issuing parent involvement regulations.

While the regulations deal in part with the more traditional activities of school districts related to parents—notification of a child's selection, establishing parent advisory councils, etc.—they also speak to other practices. Thus, it is pointed out that school districts may want to consider supporting parents by:

- informing parents of the specific instructional objectives for the child;
- reporting to the parents on each child's program;
- providing materials and suggestions to parents to help them promote the education of their children at home;
- consulting with parents about how the school can work with parents to achieve the program's objectives.

In a recent speech before the Annual Meeting of Networking Community-Based Services, Secretary Bennett stated, "Above all, I think it is now the job of the Federal government to help recreate the social and cultural fabric that used to give families support in raising children."

REFERENCES

Benson, C. S.; Medrich, E. A.; and Buckley, S. "A New View of School Efficiency: Household Time Contributions to School Achievement." *School Finance Policies and Practices*. Cambridge: Ballinger Publishing Co., 1980.

Bloom, B. S. *Developing Talent in Young People*. New York: Ballantine Books, 1985.

Bradley, R., and Caldwell, B. "Home Observation for Measurement of the Environment: A Validation Study of Screening Efficiency." *American Journal of Mental Deficiency* 81, 1977.

Boston Commission on Safe Public Schools. "Making our Schools Safer for Learning." November 1983.

Caplan, N.; Whitmore, J.; Bui, Q.; and Trautmann, M. "Scholastic Achievement Among the Children of Southeast Asian Refugees." Ann Arbor: Institute for Social Research, 1985.

Chloward, R. A., and Ohlin, L. E. *Delinquency and Opportunity: A Theory of Delinquent Gangs*. New York: Free Press, 1960.

Clark, R. M. *Family Life and School Achievement*. Chicago: University of Chicago Press, 1983.

Coleman, J. S.; Campbell, E. Q.; Hobson, D. J.; McPartland, J.; Mood, A. M.; Weinfeld, F. D.; and York, R. L. *Equality of Educational Opportunity*. Washington, D.C.: U.S. Government Printing Office, 1966.

Coleman, J. S. "Schools, Families and Children." Paper presented at the University of Chicago, April 1985.

Elkind, D. "Formal Education and Early Childhood: An Essential Difference." *Phi Delta Kappan*, May 1986.

Epstein, J. L. "Parents Reactions to Teacher Practices of Parent Involvement." *Elementary School Journal* 86, 1986.

Etzioni, A. "Self-Discipline, Schools, and the Business Community." Washington, D.C.: National Chamber Foundation, 1984.

Freeman, R. B. "Who Escapes? The Relation of Church-Going and Other Background Factors to the Socio-Economic Performance of Black Male Youths from Inner-City Poverty Tracts." Cambridge: National Bureau of Economic Research, 1985.

Gallup, A. M. "The Gallup Poll of Teachers' Attitudes Toward the Public Schools." *Phi Delta Kappan*, October 1984.

Gallup, A. M. "The 17th Annual Gallup Poll of the Public's Attitudes Toward the Public Schools." *Phi Delta Kappan*, September 1985.

Gallup, G. H. "The 15th Annual Gallup Poll of the Public's Attitudes Toward the Public Schools." *Phi Delta Kappan*, September 1983.

Goldberg, R. J. "Maternal Time Use and Preschool Performance." Paper presented in New Orleans, 1977.

Goodlad, J. I. "An Agenda for Improving Our Schools." *Executive Review* 2, May 1982.

Hanson, S. L., and Ginsburg, A. "Gaining Ground: Values and High School Success." Washington, D.C.: U.S. Department of Education, 1985.

Henderson, A. "Parent Participation—Student Achievement: The Evidence Grows." Columbia, Md.: National Committee for Citizens in Education, 1981.

Hewison, J., and Tizard J. "Parental Involvement and Reading Attainment." *British Journal of Educational Psychology* 50, 1980.

Heyns, B. *Summer Learning and the Effects of Schooling*. New York: Academic Press, 1978.

Hinckley, R. H. "Report 4: Student Home Environment, Educational Achievement, and Compensatory Education." Santa Monica: Systems Development Corp., 1979.

Honig, B. *Last Chance for Our Children*. Reading, Mass.: Addison-Wesley Publishing Co., 1985.

Iverson, B. K., and Walberg, H. J., "Home Environment and School Learning: A Quantitative Synthesis." *Journal of Environmental Education*, 1982.

Jencks, C.; Smith, M. S.; Ackland, H.; Bane, M. J.; Cohen, D.; Gintis, H.; Heyns, B.; and Michaelson, S. *Inequality: A Reassessment of the Effect of Family and Schooling in America.* New York: Basic Books, 1972.

Leibowitz, A. "Parental Inputs and Children's Achievement." *Journal of Human Resources*, 1977.

Mayeske, G. W. *A Study of the Achievement of Our Nation's Students.* Washington, D.C.: U.S. Department of Health, Education and Welfare, 1973.

Melaragno, R.; Lyons, M. F.; and Sparks, M. *Parents and Federal Education Programs, Volume 6: Title I.* Santa Monica: Systems Development Corp., 1981.

Milne, A.; Meyers, D.; Rosenthal, A.; and Ginsburg, A. "Single Parents, Working Mothers, and the Educational Achievement of School Children." *Journal of Sociology of Education*, in press.

Mosteller, F., and Moynihan, D. *On Equality of Educational Opportunity.* New York: Random House, 1972.

Myers, D. E.; Milne, A. M.; Baker, K.; and Ginsburg, A. "Student Discipline and High School Performance." Final report to the U.S. Department of Education, 1986.

National Assessment of Educational Progress. "The Reading Report Card." Washington, D.C.: National Institute of Education, 1985.

National Institute of Education. *Becoming a Nation of Readers.* Washington, D.C.: U.S. Department of Education, 1985.

National Institute of Education. *Compensatory Education Services.* Washington, D.C.: U.S. Department of Health, Education and Welfare, 1977.

National Institute of Education, "Evaluating Compensatory Education: An Interim Report on the NIE Compensatory Education Study." Washington, D.C.: NIE, 1976.

National Institute of Education. *Violent Schools—Safe Schools.* Washington, D.C.: Government Printing Office, 1978.

Polk, K., and Halferty, D. S., "Adolescence, Commitment and Delinquency." *Journal of Research in Crime and Delinquency*, 1966.

Postman, N. *Amusing Ourselves to Death: Public Discourse in the Age of Show Business.* New York: Viking Press, 1985.

Rankin, P. T., "The Relationship Between Parent Behavior and Achievement of Inner-City Elementary School Children." Paper presented at the annual meeting of the American Educational Research Association, 1967.

Rich, D. "Between Teacher and Parent." Washington, D.C.: Dorothy Rich Associates, 1985.

Rich D. *The Forgotten Factor in School Success.* Washington, D.C.: Home and School Institute, 1985.

Sava, S. G. "Dan and the Three R's." *Principal.* National Association of Elementary School Principals, March 1985.

Sewell, W., and Hauser, R. "Causes and Consequences of Higher Education: Models of the Status Attainment Process." *American Journal of Agricultural Economics* 54, 1972.

Smith, M. B. "School and Home: Focus on Achievement." *Developing Programs for the Educationally Disadvantaged.* New York: Teachers College Press, 1968.

Smith, T. E. "The Case for Parental Transmission of Educational Goals: The Importance of Accurate Offspring Perceptions." *Journal of Marriage and the Family* 44, no. 3, 1982.

Tizard, G.; Schofield, W. N.; and Hewison, J. "Collaboration Between Teachers and Parents in Assisting Children's Reading." *British Journal of Educational Psychology* 52, 1982.

U.S. Education Department. *What Works.* Washington, D.C.: U.S. Department of Education, 1986.

Walberg, H. "Improving the Productivity of America's Schools." *Educational Leadership* 41, 1984.

Walberg, H. J. "Home Environment and School Learning: Some Quantitative Models and Research Synthesis." Paper presented at the Wisconsin Research and Development Center, Madison, 1981.

Washington Research Project. "Title I of ESEA: Is It Helping Poor Children?" NAACP Legal Defense and Educational Fund, 1969.

Weiner, B. "From Each According to His Abilities: The Role of Effort in a Moral Society." *Human Development* 16, 1973.

APPENDIX B. MEGASKILLS

INTRODUCING MEGASKILLS™*

by Dorothy Rich

THE MEGASKILLS CONCEPT AND OUR CHILDREN

It is generally agreed that children need certain basic skills (usually called the three R's) in order to succeed. But, for children to learn these basic skills at school, they need to learn another important set of basics at home.

I call these "MegaSkills™." This is the curriculum that is taught at home. It's reinforced in the classroom, but mostly it has to be taught by the family.

When I think about what it really takes for children to learn and use the skills they learn, I think about attitudes and abilities that are bigger than ordinary skills. I think about confidence and motivation and problem solving and decision making. And the concept of "MegaSkills" to define these seems appropriate and right.

MegaSkills such as confidence are long-lasting, achievement-enhancing skills. They are what make possible the use of the other skills that we learn. MegaSkills are like gas to make the car go. They are the powers each one of us can have to deal constructively with the breaks in life, good and bad, and to keep on going. They are abilities to make some of our own good breaks and not wait for luck to strike.

The MegaSkills concept is a catalyst. It's like yeast, making it possible for the bread to rise. It's like a "megaphone"—designed to send the voice farther than it can ordinarily reach. That's what MegaSkills can do for the bits and pieces of learning that children acquire in school and out. MegaSkills make it possible not only for children to learn but to use that learning and to keep on learning.

---

*Adapted from *MegaSkills*™ by Dr. Dorothy Rich (Houghton Mifflin, in press). Copyright © 1987 by Dorothy Rich.

THE MEGASKILLS ROSTER

In my book, *MegaSkills*™, I explain how to start school-age children (ages 4–12) on the road to these MegaSkills through specific, easy-to-do activities:

- CONFIDENCE: feeling able to do it
- MOTIVATION: wanting to do it
- EFFORT: willing to work hard
- RESPONSIBILITY: doing what has to be done
- INITIATIVE: moving into action
- PERSEVERANCE: completing what you start
- CARING: showing concern for others
- TEAMWORK: working with others
- COMPETITION: wanting to win
- COMMON SENSE: using good judgment
- PROBLEM SOLVING: putting what you know and what you can do into action.

These aren't the only MegaSkills, but they are the ones that play a strong role in determining success in school and beyond.

SPECIAL IMPORTANCE
OF THE MEGASKILLS CONCEPT TODAY

There is justifiable concern about American education today and whether our children are learning enough and working hard enough. The remarkable school success of recently arrived Asian immigrant children has prompted questions about what these children have that American youngsters don't have.

What American children must have are abilities that include reading, writing, and math—but that also go beyond them. We know that while it is essential—a given—to be able to read, it is not enough.

The problem is not that our children don't learn how to read. They do. Educational research has confirmed that most of our children do learn the basics of reading and math in the early

91

grades. What happens is that many children do not keep on reading and wanting to learn more.

I want to enable families to help children not only acquire basics but go beyond them to get on the road to being a learner for life. This learning starts early and it starts at home.

No school is an island. The job of the school is to teach; the job of the home is to help students use what they have been taught so that the school is surrounded by a community of learning, of enthusiasm and support.

THE NEVER-ENDING REPORT CARD

MegaSkills are on every report card, often in the areas called "citizenship" or "level of effort." And they are on all job performance evaluations. We're graded on MegaSkills all through life. Look at these examples:

Report Card

- Displays self-confidence
- Is willing to take risks
- Completes work independently
- Understands and applies new concepts
- Is responsive
- Demonstrates self-control
- Concentrates on work
- Masters new materials and techniques
- Values quality of work
- Shows courtesy and consideration
- Maintains a sense of fair play

Job Performance Evaluation

- Shows ability and willingness to make decisions
- Demonstrates ability and willingness to solve problems
- Delegates responsibility or authority as applicable
- Has integrity
- Shows common sense and perspective

- Has knowledge and technical skills
- Completes assignments
- Shows ability to work with people
- Maintains positive personal relationships

Children aren't born with MegaSkills. They learn them, and parents and teachers teach them, not all at once, and not perfectly, but little by little, day-by-day.

A PARENT'S HOPE: A NATION'S NEED

All parents and teachers want children who are smart, motivated, responsible, cooperative, good listeners, and contributors who have self-confidence and self-discipline. This is no small order. Coincidentally, these are the very qualities this nation needs in its citizens now and for the next century—leaders who can and who want to keep learning.

So, how do we do it, especially today? I urge that we *do* it by teaching MegaSkills and that every family and every teacher *can* do it. I know from experience with thousands of teachers and parents across the country that I can help families be better teachers of children. What parents must learn is how to take advantage of their own strengths. What they will be teaching is that children also have strengths and responsibilities. Children will learn that hard work and perseverance and self-discipline are not only worthwhile but also give them pleasure and self-satisfaction now and later.

TOMORROW IS NOT FAR AWAY

When children come home from school, parents ask, "What did you do in school today?" The typical answer, even from talkative kids, is "nothing." Parents need to keep asking that question anyway, but to have another, bigger question in mind.

The bigger question is: "What did you learn today that you will be able to make use of tomorrow?" Children will not be able to answer this, but it's vital that parents begin thinking about this critical question now. It's a question that has everything to do with children's success, in school and out.

The academic term for this is "transfer." Thinking is transfer: it's taking a fact or a set of facts and a situation and putting them together to try to solve a problem. It's making a decision based on what we learn and what we anticipate will happen in the future.

Education to be useful for the 1990s and beyond has got to transfer. MegaSkills make learning transfer possible. Little is really known now about what specific skills will be needed for the twenty-first century. We don't know the situations our children will face or even the machines they will use.

What we do know for sure is that our children will have to be able to transfer what they learn today. They need lifelong, knowledge-enhancing skills, good any year, and any place. That's what MegaSkills are all about.

Note on MegaSkills™ Workshops: To provide this program to families across the country, beyond those who can purchase the book, the author has designed a series of MegaSkills™ workshops that school systems, churches and community centers will be able to obtain and sponsor in localities everywhere. For more information on these workshops and the training that will be available to those who want to lead these programs, contact Dorothy Rich directly at the Home and School Institute (Special Projects Office, 1201 16th Street, NW, Washington, DC 20036).

APPENDIX C. MEETING DIFFERENT FAMILY NEEDS

A VARIETY OF PARENT INVOLVEMENT PROGRAMS

Schools need to consider different kinds of programs to meet differing family involvement needs. Below is a listing of Home and School Institute (HSI) programs that illustrate the spectrum of programs that need to be considered in addressing family involvement issues. They help answer the questions: What do our teachers need? What do our parents want? How can both groups be served?

1. *Academic and Personal Skills Development*
   This is a general academic and personal skills development program used for a wide and diverse group of families interested in helping to enhance their children's learning abilities.

2. *Bilingual Program (English/Spanish)*
   This program is for limited-English-proficient parents to involve them in educationally supportive activities with their children at home, including academic and American-culture survival skills/activities.

3. *Career Development*
   This program enables families to help their young teenagers gain the positive skills and attitudes that will enhance their ability to get and keep jobs.

4. *Family Learning Centers*
   This is a program for a site within the community, such as a library, that offers information and activities for parents and children about the family as educator.

© 1987 by the Home and School Institute.

5. *Family Literacy*

This two-tiered (parent and child) program provides information and parenting skills for adults while simultaneously providing academic skills development for children.

6. *Intergenerational Program*

This program involves senior citizens in an educational team effort with families to enhance the academic and motivational achievement of children.

7. *Single-Parent Support—Workplace/Home Connection*

This program provides special support for single parents working to meet the special demands they face to maintain strong family life and to enhance the educational achievement of their children.

INSIDE THE HOME AND SCHOOL INSTITUTE LEARNING SYSTEM

Teachers will find it valuable to "see" inside a typical Home and School Institute School-to-Home Learning System. A complete kit of materials, the system is designed to give teachers everything needed to conduct a semester-long school-to-home program.

Sample Table of Contents

DATA FROM THE FIELD:
WHAT TEACHERS AND PARENTS SAY

What is known about the impact of such school-to-home programs? Are they worth the effort? What do teachers and parents say? It is useful to review the following data from Home and School Institute programs, as they have been ongoing since 1964. The following points are supported by the cumulative evidence of data collected on projects implemented across grades K-8 in 20 states.

1. Families use the materials. Participation rates are consistently high at all sites.
2. Families report they find activities beneficial and enjoy doing them.
3. Teachers find programs contribute to improved student attitudes and behaviors in the classroom.
4. Teachers say programs foster more and better communications with parents.
5. Program activities contribute to improved skills and academic achievement.

Teacher-Parent Partnership—NEA-sponsored project in 17 states, 1985–ongoing
The core of the project consists of learning activities third graders and their parents complete at home together. Activities do not duplicate schoolwork and are designed to build discipline, improve study habits, and enhance thinking skills. In 1985, family completion rates across sites ranged from 33 to 70 percent. Data show:

- 99 percent of PARENTS surveyed would recommend project activities to other parents.
- 98 percent believe children learned something useful.
- 97 percent said activities helped them spend enjoyable time with their children.

- 88 percent of TEACHERS said program would be useful to other teachers.

- 38 percent reported children seemed more responsible in completing homework.
- 48 percent reported parents showed increased interest in school.
- 54 percent said program enhanced image of teachers in their communities.

In Any Language: Parents Are Teachers, Arlington, VA, 1983–85

This multicultural, multilingual parent-involvement program was designed to provide practice in English for limited-English-proficiency elementary and middle school students. Activities in English and target languages cover practical topics about daily life activities. Data show:

- Participation rates ranged from 94 to 79 percent in 1984; 84 to 61 percent in 1985.
- TEACHERS reported parents became more involved in child's school experience.
- Percentage of families participating voluntarily ranged from 94.5 to 79 percent.
- PARENT comments on weekly feedback sheets were highly favorable.

The Senior Corps Home-School Volunteer Program, Washington, DC, 1982–85

This home learning program involves senior citizens working with special education junior high school students and their families. Subject matter of activities is reading, math, and health/home economics. Data show:

- 100 percent of SENIORS enjoyed their participation and wanted to continue.
- 90 percent of STUDENTS said they liked working with senior citizens.
- 86 percent of PARENTS reported improvement in their children's schoolwork.
- ALL SCHOOL PRINCIPALS said project benefited students and had value for the school.

- 71 percent of TEACHERS indicated program made improvement in skills of students and had positive effect on classroom attitude, behavior, attendance, and motivation.
- 100 percent of teachers said they would participate again and would recommend project.

The Family Learning Place—Special Education Project,
Washington, DC, 1980–83

In this adaptation of the HSI model for children with learning disabilities, inner-city students in grades 2-6 identified as performing substantially below grade level participated. The model was keyed to visual, aural, and perceptual learning modalities. Data show:

- TEACHERS reported a significant increase in children's reasoning and visual-aural skills.
- Majority of students participating in project were mainstreamed.
- More than half the children improved their attitudes toward school and in relationships with adults.
- PARENTS said project contributed to children's school achievement and improved skills.

Families Learning Together, Landrum, SC, 1978–79

This program provided simultaneous adult and child learning in basic skills. It served a population of rural families with children in grades K-6. Participation rate was 77 percent of total school population. Data show:

- 98 percent of PARENTS said they learned useful skills and knowledge from program.
- 98.5 percent said they felt more confident in working with child in home.

- TEACHERS said families became more aware of their educational role:
  —"Parents are spending more time listening to children and helping them."

101

—"Students are showing more enthusiasm and doing home-work more often."

—"Children like school better and show an improved self-image."

Project AHEAD, Los Angeles, 1978-continuing

This parent-to-parent approach begun for the Southern Christian Leadership Conference West serves Black and Hispanic children from low income neighborhoods. Results showed significant increase in test scores.

- 97 percent of PARENTS indicated they wanted their children to continue in the program, which has now been adopted by the Los Angeles Unified School District.

Project HELP, Benton Harbor, MI, 1977-81

This program was designed to serve children of low income and migrant workers. In the beginning, children had lowest scores of all groups in school system. After program of HSI learning activities sent home weekly, youngsters made gains in reading equal to those of groups that started at higher level.

Doctoral Study, Washington, DC and suburbs, 1974-75

This initial field test for the HSI Home-School Education System was conducted in eight first grades in inner city and suburbs. HSI project children scored significantly higher on standardized reading tests than control group.

APPENDIX D. CHARACTERISTICS OF EFFECTIVE FAMILIES

Note: Teachers will find the following article helpful to share with parents.

EFFECTIVE FAMILIES HELP CHILDREN SUCCEED IN SCHOOL*

by Reginald M. Clark

Over the last few years, a number of urban school systems have focused on developing school characteristics which can help raise the achievement levels of poor and minority children. Led by the late Ron Edmonds, followers of the "effective schools" movement found that when schools are warm, nurturing places with high expectations for all students, every child can learn—regardless of family income or background.

Most of my own research has focused on families and their relationships with schools—equally important ingredients in school success. We all know the grim statistics for low-income Black and Hispanic students. Less than half graduate with their class from high school, and many who do lack the basic skills needed to do college level academic work and support independent households. Conventional wisdom says that the crime-ridden neighborhoods and unstable homes these students live in are greatly to blame for their failure. What I have been more interested in is why some students do succeed in school in the face of such living conditions—and there are some. Even in pubic housing, in single-parent households, in the homes of the unemployed and working poor,

---

some students stand out as well-motivated high achievers. What makes the difference for these children?

I have spent a decade in research trying to find the answer to that question. In one study of 12th grade Black students, I selected 16 households in three low-income Chicago neighborhoods. Some students had good grades, high achievement test scores and strong recommendations from their teachers. Others had poor achievement by the same measures. Some of the high achievers as well as low achievers lived in single-parent households. In a separate study of 4th graders from Los Angeles, I selected 32 students from varied ethnic backgrounds (nearly half were Mexican-American and 8 were Caucasian). Their family structures and income levels were diverse. As before, some had high achievement levels and others low. My graduate students and I went into their homes asking, why do some of these students succeed and others fail? The answers I came out with were related to family lifestyle. The high-achieving students came from "effective families."

Like effective schools, effective families have a set of easy-to-identify characteristics. These cut across family income, education, and ethnic background. They remain true for single- and two-parent households and for families with working and nonworking mothers. Effective families display a number of positive attitudes and behaviors toward their children which help them succeed in school and life.

As I questioned family members and observed their daily life together, one thing became clear: effective families believe they can make a difference in their children's academic and personal development. They do not feel overwhelmed by their circumstances. They feel in control of their lives. Even when they live in poverty, effective families keep a hopeful, optimistic outlook. Unlike many other families in similar circumstances, they do not sit around feeling sorry for themselves. They not only listen attentively to the problems of their own children, they have time for others. Consequently, their homes are often perceived as a safe place to gather for support and understanding.

Effective families have a dream of family success, a vision of personal success for each child and a plan for making their dreams come true. The key to success, effective parents tell their children, is individual effort. It is not fate or genes or good looks that make the differences but old-fashioned hard work. Children in effective families believe that success will come from their own inner motivation and commitment to an achievement-oriented ("go for it!") lifestyle.

The dream that most effective families contemplate combines good health and material well-being (a good job, nice house, car and clothes) with an active spiritual life and service to the community. Parents discuss with their children specific steps they can take both now and in the future to realize their dream of a better life. Getting a good education is a major part of their strategy.

Effective parents start early to build their child's self-confidence, self-control, and self-esteem. They provide lots of verbal support, using endearing nicknames, praising children's skills and efforts ("good job," "you're okay"), and telling them they love them. When they talk with their children, it is with a spirit of warmth, admiration, and respect. They tell their youngsters about the strength and good that comes from being a "good learner."

Effective parents treat their children as winners. Even when a child makes a mistake, he or she is not made to feel like a loser. Effective parents know when to let children be the center of attention in a group. This helps them learn a healthy kind of self-love without becoming conceited or "full of themselves."

Effective families see themselves as a mutual support system. From early years, every child is given some household responsibility appropriate to his/her age which makes the child feel important to the family. In single-parent and working-parent families, older brothers and sisters often take the role of parental advisors to younger children.

Effective families have clearly understood standards and household rules which are enforced consistently—but parents put more energy into finding worthwhile learning activities for children than into keeping children in line.

In the effective families I have visited, children were engaged in learning activities 25-35 hours a week. Some of these hours are quiet time devoted to homework or leisure time reading, but these families view learning more broadly. Hobbies, games, household chores, part-time jobs, sports, organized youth programs, family outings, even creative daydreaming provide opportunities for learning. When effective parents watch television with their children, they discuss which situations are true to life and which are fantasy.

Effective parents discourage idleness and help channel children's time into wholesome activities. They know where they are and who they are with. They help children avoid peer pressure to use drugs or engage in criminal activities. They also help their children develop relationships with other children who have equally high achievement goals.

Part of the effective family's overall learning plan is frequent contact with each child's teacher to check on school progress. Effective parents work cooperatively with teachers and ask what home learning activities can complement work performed in school.

Effective families encourage the spiritual growth of each child. Parents stress each person's need to satisfy their own inner needs, then go on to use talents and energies to help others. They inspire children to strive for inner peace and love. They help them gain the strength to overcome fears and work through the conflicts and stresses of life.

"SPONSORED INDEPENDENCE" IS AN EFFECTIVE PARENTING STYLE

Taken together, these positive attitudes and behaviors engender the self-confidence and build the self-esteem which children need to achieve in school. I call this lifestyle "sponsored independence." It involves making a lifelong commitment to each child, ranging from caring for physical needs and emotional well-being in early years to advocating publicly for a child in schools and with other institutions as the need arises. The parent who authoritatively "sponsors" his child maintains authority in the household, without being authoritarian. The same parent eases each child toward independence as she matures, without being overly permissive and without making the child feel intimidated.

Other researchers have reached similar conclusions about parenting style and school achievement. Diana Baumrind of the University of California-Berkeley and Sanford Dornbusch of Stanford University call the effective style "authoritative." It is characterized by involving children in family decision making, praising good grades, and offering help and encouragement. It is more effective in raising school achievement than either an authoritarian or permissive approach to parenting.

10 CHARACTERISTICS OF EFFECTIVE FAMILIES

Whether you call their style "authoritative" or "sponsored independence," effective families have these characteristics:

1. a feeling of control over their lives
2. frequent communication of high expectations to children
3. a family dream of success for the future
4. hard work as a key to success
5. an active, not a sedentary lifestyle
6. 25-35 home-centered learning hours per week
7. the family viewed as a mutual support system and problem-solving unit
8. clearly understood household rules, consistently enforced
9. frequent contact with teachers
10. emphasis on spiritual growth

How would you rate your own family's performance? How would you rate the effectiveness of most families in your child's school? If you work through a parent-teacher organization or school council, you might use this checklist to develop support activities for families in your attendance area.

Reginald M. Clark is a California educator, researcher, author, and program consultant to private and public agencies interested in home-school collaboration. He is the author of Family Life and School Achievement: Why Poor Black Children Succeed or Fail.

BIBLIOGRAPHY

1. Barth, R. "Parents as Helpers, Critics, and Adversaries." *National Elementary Principal* 58, no. 1 (October 1979): 52.

2. Bronfenbrenner, U. *Is Early Intervention Effective? A Report on Longitudinal Evaluations of Preschool Programs*. Vol. 2. Washington, D.C.: Department of Health, Education, and Welfare, 1974.

3. Bureau of the Census. *Statistical Abstract of the United States*. Washington, D.C.: Bureau of Labor Statistics, 1985; p. 399.

4. Burks, Gladys E. "An Analysis of the Cost Effectiveness of Title I Pull-Out Instruction in the Benton Harbor Area Schools." Benton Harbor, Michigan, Schools, 1978.

5. Burns, J. *The Study of Parental Involvement in Four Federal Education Programs: Executive Summary*. Washington, D.C.: Department of Education, Office of Planning, Budget and Evaluation, 1982.

6. Clark, Reginald. *Family Life and School Achievement: Why Poor Black Children Succeed or Fail*. Chicago: University of Chicago Press, 1983.

7. Compton, Nancy; Duncan, Mara; Hruska, Jack. *How Schools Can Help Combat Student Pregnancy*. Washington, D.C.: National Education Association, 1987.

8. Dave, R. J. "The Identification and Measurement of Environment Process Variables That Are Related to Educational Achievement." Ph.D. dissertation, University of Chicago, 1963.

9. Epstein, Joyce. *Effects on Parents of Teacher Practices in Parent Involvement*. Baltimore: Center for Social Organization of Schools, Johns Hopkins University, 1984.

10. Espinoza, R. *Work and Family Life Among Anglo, Black and Mexican-American Single-Parent Families: Executive Summary*. Austin, Tex.: Southwest Educational Development Laboratory, 1983.

11. Goodson, B., and Hess, R. *Parents as Teachers of Young Children: An Evaluative Review of Some Contemporary Concepts and Programs.* Palo Alto, Calif: Stanford University, 1975.

12. Gordon, I.; Olmsted, P.; Rubin R.; and True, J. *Continuity Between Home and School: Aspects of Parent Involvement in Follow Through.* Chapel Hill, N.C.: University of North Carolina Press, 1978.

13. Gotts, E. *Summary of Report: Characteristics of Families with Special Needs in Relation to Schools.* Charleston, W. Va.: Appalachia Educational Laboratory, 1982.

14. Hetherington, E. M. "Children and Divorce." Paper presented at annual meeting of American Psychological Association, New York, 1979.

15. Hetherington, E. M.; Featherman, D. L.; and Camara, K. A. "Intellectual Functioning and Achievement of Children in One-Parent Households." Paper prepared for National Institute of Education, Washington, D.C., 1981.

16. Home and School Institute. *Families Learning Together.* Washington, D.C.: the Institute, 1979.

17. _____. *Final Report: Parent-School Partnership Project.* Washington, D.C.: Department of Education, 1983.

18. _____. *Conference Report: Single-Parent Families and the Schools—Opportunity or Crisis?* Washington, D.C.: the Institute, 1984.

19. Knowles, M. S. *The Adult Learner: A Neglected Species.* Houston: Gould Publishing, 1978.

20. Levine, Michael P. *How Schools Can Help Combat Student Eating Disorders: Anorexia Nervosa and Bulimia.* Washington, D.C.: National Education Association, 1987.

21. Moles, O. "Trends in Divorce and Effects on Children." Paper presented at meeting of American Academy for the Advancement of Science, Washington, D.C., 1982.

22. National Commission on Excellence in Education. *A Nation at Risk: The Imperative for Education Reform.* Washington, D.C.: the Commission, 1983.

23. National Education Association. *Nationwide Teacher Opinion Poll, 1983*. Washington, D.C.: the Association, 1983.

24. _____. "Report on Teacher-Parent Partnership Project." Washington, D.C.: the Association, 1985.

25. National Education Association, and Home and School Institute. *Teacher-Parent Partnership*. Washington, D.C.: the Association and the Institute, 1985.

26. Phi Delta Kappa. *Gallup Polls of Attitudes Toward Education, 1969-84*. Bloomington, Ind.: Phi Delta Kappa, 1984.

27. Plaskett, Bernard. *AHEAD Report* (Accelerating Home Education and Development). Los Angeles: Southern Christian Leadership Conference West, 1978.

28. Rich, Dorothy. *The Forgotten Factor in School Success—The Family*. Washington, D.C.: Home and School Institute, 1985.

29. Rich, Dorothy; Mattox, B.; and Van Dien, J. "Building on Family Strengths: The 'Nondeficit' Involvement Model for Teaming Home and School." *Educational Leadership* (April 1979): 506-10.

30. Tower, Cynthia Crosson. *How Schools Can Help Combat Child Abuse and Neglect*. 2d ed. Washington, D.C.: National Education Association, 1987.

31. Towers, Richard L. *How Schools Can Help Combat Student Drug and Alcohol Abuse*. Washington, D.C.: National Education Association, 1987.

32. Trinity College. *Interim Report: Trinity/Arlington Teacher and Parent Training for School Success Project*. Washington, D.C.: Department of Education, Bilingual Education Office, 1984.

33. Walberg, Herbert. "Families as Partners in Educational Productivity." *Phi Delta Kappan* 65, no. 6 (1984): 397-400.

34. Wallerstein, J. S., and Kelly, J. B. *Surviving the Breakup: How Children and Parents Cope with Divorce*. New York: Basic Books, 1980.

35. Williams, D. L. *Parent Involvement in Education: What A Survey Reveals*. Austin, Tex.: Southwest Educational Development Laboratory, 1984.

Family / Community Materials
Available from NEA

Schools and Parents United: A Practical Approach to Student Success

Schools and Families: Issues and Actions
by Dorothy Rich

Teachers and Parents: An Adult-to-Adult Approach
by Dorothy Rich

A Guide and Plan for Conducting 12 Workshops for Schools and Parents United: A Practical Aproach to Student Success developed by the Home and School Institute, Inc. (includes 28 Workshop Handouts)

Home Learning Recipes for Parents and Their Children (K–3)
Home Learning Recipes for Parents and Their Children (Grades 4–5)
Home Learning Recipes for Parents and Their Children (Grades 6–8)
Home Learning Recipes for Parents and Their Teenagers (Grades 9–12)
(4 reproduction masters)

Family-School Educational Partnership
Focus: Family Involvement in Action
(2 videotapes)

Schools and Families Working Together
Teachers Working with Parents
(2 filmstrips)

Briefing for Parents Filmstrips

Helping Your Child Grow Up
Helping Your Child in School
How to Listen to Your Child and
    How to Get Your Child to Listen to You
Parent-Teacher Conferences
Parental Discipline
Reading Is Around Us
What Can You Do to Help Your Child Succeed?